"'You can't change,' is certainly the biggest, Sata.. ....
ever hear. Thank you for challenging that lie that so many are certain is
true and are scared to even dare question. God bless you Thom for your
thoughtful and challenging words."

-- *Stan*

"Your message reminds me of Christ's words, 'The truth shall set you free.'
(John 8:31) He is really the one who sets us free, but He cannot do it when
we hide behind lies. Those who comfort the broken with lies are really
imprisoning them. 'This is going to hurt. So let's get it done' is a much
better message. Down-to-earth. Honest."

-- *Inge*

"Thank you, Thom. I've read your recent writings on your blog. They were
very powerful and empowering thoughts and most insightful. The Lord
has a quite amazing way of feeding us encouragement and comfort. I am
blessed to have read this. I feel I am not the only one."

-- *Odd Bloke Out*

"Thanks for the good word, and for having the willingness to speak truth
into the lives of men and woman who so desperately need it in a world of
relative values and instant gratification."

-- *Bret*

"What a powerful article. I just found you but I will be back to read more.
I know that it must be very painful to bare your past sins in this manner
but I commend you for your courage and your sincerity. I pray that others
will be helped by your struggles."

-- *Zohar*

"My husband and I so poignantly know and relate to your words. Voices
like yours are so hard to come by. Thank you for your clarity, your
eloquence, and your gentle nudges to the mainstream church. We are
grateful recipients of the new attitude of grace and compassion as we
heal."

-- *Cori*

"God really spoke to me in your blog about hiding from Him. Thank you so much for this wonderful encouragement."

-- Anonymous

"Wow this is something I really needed to read. I am finally slowly starting to get the courage to share my burden of SSA with others after many years of shame, guilt, and hiding. I have not had the courage to go through with it yet but this reaffirmed to me that it's something God wants me to do even though I am afraid to do it. This was an encouragement to me."

-- AJ

"Thanks for sharing about the depth of God's grace, which always goes past our sin. You are an encouragement!"

-- Jen

"Thom, I am at a loss for words on how to respond to such a simple and concise delivery of your message, couched in humility and wrapped in love."

-- Daemon

"I've seldom read anything so beautiful and meaningful in my entire life. It seems you somehow got inside me to re-ignite some of my candles. God bless you and your personal ministry."

-- Anonymous

"Thanks for having the courage to face your struggles, and share yourself with others through your writing."

-- D

SURVIVING SEXUAL
BROKENNESS

- WHAT GRACE CAN DO -

THOM HUNTER

WESTBOW
PRESS
A DIVISION OF THOMAS NELSON

WestBow Press books may be ordered through booksellers or by contacting:

WestBow Press
A Division of Thomas Nelson
1663 Liberty Drive
Bloomington, IN 47403
www.westbowpress.com
1-(866) 928-1240

ISBN: 978-1-4497-0731-6 (sc)
ISBN: 978-1-4497-0817-7 (hc)
ISBN: 978-1-4497-0818-4 (e)

Library of Congress Control Number: 2010939774

Printed in the United States of America

WestBow Press rev. date: 11/12/2010

And the God of all grace, who called you to His eternal glory in Christ, after you have suffered a little while, will Himself restore you and make you strong, firm and steadfast.

1 Peter 5:10

THANK YOU ----------------

During this sometimes lonely, very lengthy, often frightening, and frequently discouraging walk, two persons never left my side. The first, of course is Christ, who first loved me.

The other is my wife.

So I dedicate this book and the remaining years of my life to my wife, Lisa, who has never left my side and has proven the truth that love endures much, suffers much, always hopes, and rejoices in the truth. Lisa is amazing and her love bears all. God heard her relentless prayers.

Others have walked with me – those who sat with me and listened to me and endured with me – at First Stone Ministries in Oklahoma City, in particular the unwavering Stephen Black.

I am thankful for everyone that has remained in my life through this struggle.

CONTENTS

INTRODUCTION

While it's probably not a good thing to get too bogged down in the "who am I?" and the "who are you?" questions, they do come up in our minds every now and then. We can't help it.

Who am I? Who are you? God only knows. But, thank God, God truly *does* know.

It took me a long time to admit I was "sexually-broken." I knew from an early age that engaging in sexual activity with a person of the same sex was wrong. I knew it instinctively, but I also knew it spiritually. God's Word was clear on the issue. Still, it seemed impossible to resist and yielding to it cost me greatly. Only by accepting the fact that I was "broken," could I accept my need for repair, through a desire for holiness.

Born of insecurity, my issue was homosexuality, but many Christians and non-Christians struggle with other forms of sexual brokenness: pornography addiction, lust, adultery, idolatry, addictive masturbation. What was meant for good – our sexuality – has been corrupted in many ways by our hearts seeking solace in so many wrong places. Still, those of us who know Christ will always hope to replace our brokenness with wholeness though holiness. It is a survivable struggle.

I was not always sexually broken.

I was the little boy who sat on a sidewalk and watched the ants cross by, inches in front of my bare feet and wondered why they had so many to "be with." My father had left the family and we were splintered to the point of co-mingled solitude. *God knew me in my aloneness.*

I was the second-grader zipped into a camping tent with a pedophile, innocent one in the hands of a not-so . . . being changed without my knowledge or consent and certainly in ways I could not understand. *God knew me in my vulnerability.*

I was the shy middle-schooler envying the boys rising in popularity and athletic prowess, wondering why I was uncomfortable and so uncertain of self. *God knew me in my awkwardness.*

I was the high-schooler anxious to move on beyond the presence of peers and the pressures of performance, but totally unsure as to what I was moving to. *God knew me in my uncertainty.*

I was the college freshman exploring freedom, walking in the dark on a misty campus and accepting an invitation from a stranger into a new world that slyly presented itself as an answer to all my confusion. *God knew me in my stumbling.*

I became the man hiding behind the man, developing the double-mind, fencing in the soul, projecting the persona, erecting the image, avoiding the reality, feeding the brokenness of the past so it could bleed into the present and project into the future. *God knew me in my destructiveness.*

In the timeless view of God, I am all of those described above . . . but so much more. In God's expansive view of time . . . I am broken *and* whole, hurt *and* healed.

The weight of who I am is not a burden to an omniscient loving God whose grace covers all.

I am the man who is healing, rejecting society's claims of inevitability, shaking off judgment, refusing to surrender to others' genetic wishful thinking, accepting the reality of choice and embracing the simplicity of daily surrender . . . to the God who *always* knew me.

> *What is man that You are mindful of him, the son of man that You care for him? -- Psalm 8:4*

We are who we are in part because of where we've been. In all those places, God was "mindful" of us. We hid; we paused; we ran; we rejected; we fell. Sometimes we ran to Him; sometimes we fell before Him; sometimes we cried out to Him; sometimes we pleaded with Him. In all ways, He is always "mindful."

I am a husband and a father. I have five children who are: a business owner, a graduate student, an Army Ranger, a police officer, a college student. I have four daughters-in-law and seven grandchildren. I have two dogs and five fish. I have a wife who has loved me from before "I do" and still does.

I am all of the things I mentioned above: sometimes alone, sometimes vulnerable, sometimes awkward, sometimes uncertain, sometimes stumbling, and sometimes destructive. I am also healing; I am surrendering;

I am changing. I am showing the signs of the struggle, which means I do not yield to brokenness as inevitable or final.

Maybe you . . . or someone you love . . . is a bit like me, too-long bent beneath the weight of who we are, ready to let the God who bears all . . . bear us.

It's tragic how many things in life we do for love and acceptance, and yet all that time we have Someone who loves us and accepts us from the moment we are conceived. It's sorrowful that we yearn for someone to really know us and yet we have always had Someone who has always known the very number of hairs on our head. It's sad that we want so not to be alone and we have always had Someone who said He would never leave us. And yet, even if we are aware of His presence, we often try to hide ourselves.

When I look back - - - which it is getting easier to do — I understand much more clearly what use to be not so comforting.

And we know that God causes all things to work together for good to those who love God, to those who are called according to His purpose. -- Romans 8:28

The truth is, if we believe that we can find our own way out of this wilderness of sin, we won't. It is in Christ alone. Still, Christ is not limited in His workings and can use anything or anyone He so chooses to bring the lost sheep back into the flock.

I had done many things right and well. I married the woman I loved; I tried very hard to be a good father to my five children, though there is no doubt they were damaged by the deep secrets in my life . . . secrets kept from them in part to protect them and in part to feed my own personal misguided search to fill an emptiness only God can fill.

I never abandoned church. I never turned my back on God's Word. I was not totally hopeless, but often futilely helpless.

Just as my journey began in the hands of a twisted man who robbed me of my trust in all men . . . my journey's end began in the hands of men I learned to trust. These are men who fear God but were themselves fearless in the face of my confusion, caring enough to be a steady hand through my continued stumbling, rather than recoiling in horror as if I bore a sin of contagion. These men straight-forwardly helped me to right myself, presenting me with supportive accountability, not super-scriptural checklists. Through these relationships, I learned the power of compassionate truth from men who had ears to hear and hearts big enough to carry the burdens I finally unloaded. And they wanted nothing from me other than to see me walk steadily towards freedom.

Myself long suspicious of God – particularly when told to view Him as Father – I began to experience God's love through people who approached me as God-with-skin-on, yielded to His purpose, enabled with the stamina it takes to walk faithfully at the side of one who had teetered so often on the edge.

For me, this has not been an easy struggle. No bright light switched on in my brain to chase away the darkness in my soul. It took practical and persistent help from people trained to do so . . . and it took a willingness to lose all in the pursuit of freedom. Through the help of a professional counselor, I addressed the empty spaces of my past that had been filled in wicked ways. Through the Living Waters program at First Stone Ministries in Oklahoma City, with the help of fellow strugglers, I addressed my present and began to see that the future is not written in stone, but built on the Rock.

While most people in my life – from my own children to most of my church friends --wearied of this hill-and-valley plagued journey, a few did not. Perhaps God just considered them strong enough to bear it all . . . or perhaps they were perfectly gifted for the walk. They know who they are because they never turned away.

Perhaps the greatest help comes from those who remain at our side, even though they receive pressure from others to remove themselves from the life of the struggler, supposedly for the struggler's own good, as if abandonment and rejection were akin to shock therapy. The peddlers of hopelessness shake their heads at the stalwart ones who stand. My wife endured this out of her love for me and her belief that God's will was for her to stay and see what God could do.

For some, the big question is . . . how can a marriage survive such a huge failing as this, such deception, such pain, unfaithfulness, distortion and mistrust? And some marriages don't. Mine did. Through the grace of God and the adopted grace of Lisa, my wife, who has the ability to see through Jesus' eyes. She understands the price He paid and let it serve as an example for a price she would pay herself in hope. And, she, who had more reason than anyone to abandon me . . . rescued me instead.

If we are willing, God brings rescuers into our lives. And if we are willing, He can take us from the brink of disaster and call us to become rescuers ourselves. Those who have seen the pit know best where to place the warning signs to help others avoid the fall.

I had a hard time believing that some of the things that happened to me - - - as well as some of the things I myself did - - - could possibly be used by God for any good purpose. Now I know better.

I know there is always more going on than I can possibly understand, so I am learning to stand on God's promises.

God loves me even when I can't feel it.

God is working in every moment even when I can't see it.

God is changing me even when I don't understand it.

God has always been there, no matter how rejected I felt by others, no matter how hard I was rejecting Him.

When I was knit in my mother's womb . . . God was there.

When my Dad drove away for the final time . . . God was there.

When the scoutmaster crawled into my tent . . . God was there.

When I married my best friend . . . God was there.

When my children were born . . . God was there.

When they turned away from me . . . God was there.

When I was hurt . . . God was there.

When I hurt others . . . God was there.

When I was redeemed . . . God was there.

When I fell . . . God was there.

When I was restored . . . God was there.

When I got up this morning . . . God was there.

When I lay down this evening . . . God will be there.

And when I ascend into heaven . . . God will be there too.

There is no secret too buried . . . no past too dark . . . no confusion too deep . . . no sin too ugly . . . no inner or outer fault so distasteful that it is above the enduring and ever-present grace of God. Nothing can separate us from our Father's love.

There is no struggle He cannot cease.

CHAPTER 1

WHICH FACE WILL
FINISH THE RACE?

Through love and truth, restored to stand, renewed and clean within,
My past forgiven, my present new, my future freed from secret sin,
I am at peace with where I am; forgiveness lets me breath again,
The dark is gone, the ropes untied, the light of grace has entered in.

He set me free because He lives.
I am . . . I can . . . because . . . He is.

But where I am is not enough; to linger in this peaceful place
Of solitude and healing, of redemption, cleansed through grace.
He asks and prods that those who change quicken then the pace
Of moving forward, not alone, but with others in the race.

He set me free because He lives.
I am . . . I can . . . because . . . He is.

-- Thom Hunter

When I was a little boy in Texas, yearning for a summer snow cone . . . and broke, there was only one solution: Coke bottles. Well, not just Coke bottles, but Nehi grape bottles and 7-Up bottles and Big Red bottles and Dr. Pepper bottles. I'd start under the kitchen sink first and claim any I could find there. Then I would walk the neighborhood and the nearby park. Each bottle could be redeemed for a few cents at the U-Totem convenience store. Pick 'em up, haul 'em in, get your cash and spend it. A snow cone, some Sweet-Tarts, maybe even a Spiderman comic book on a good day.

Sometimes the discarded bottles would have spiders in them or be filled with dirt, or, even worse, might have been used by a tobacco-chewer for a spit receptacle. I never gave a lot of thought to the fact that, post-redemption, those same bottles would be filled again and back on the grocery shelves. Redeemed. Clean and clear and filled with purpose.

Some of the bottles I found were too chipped or too cracked to be redeemed. They made good targets for a BB gun or, usually, just got tossed back down and left behind. Unredeemed. Beyond use now.

They were just bottles.

But what about people? Are we sifting through the discarded, searching for "The Most Likely to Be Redeemed," like we did "Most Likely to Succeed" in high school? Do we vote with our eyes and actions, tossing aside a few that are just a little too broken to be of further use? Are we sealing someone's future because of the revealing of his past?

I have a past. Cracks and chips and broken pieces. Dirt.

When I am still and focused, I try to see that past as God sees it in his way of flowing time where past and present and future meld into just being. Where was and is and still-to-be are . . . one. And I see a little boy, a struggling teen, a stumbling man and . . . I know them. Indeed, when I try really hard to see all three as God does . . . I even *like* them. I see them in snapshots, first with an old black-and-white Polaroid, then a Kodak Instamatic, then in digital brilliance. A little boy with a burr . . . a kid with a cowlick . . . a teen with shaggy hair on his shoulders . . . a man with graying thinness. Snap . . . snap . . . blink.

Still, as Clarence, the angel in "It's a Wonderful Life," said when focusing in on the face of good old George Bailey, "I like that face." I agree . . . those faces, all mine; I like them now.

Still, like them as I do, I find myself, when viewing through the continuum of time and memory, wanting to warn them . . . to say a lot of "don'ts." To freeze the frame. To reach down and move them like a plastic piece on a game board. It hurts to see where they are heading, but I cannot intervene. I think I understand a little bit how God must grieve.

Don't go there.
Don't do that.
Don't open that door.
Don't close that door.
Don't tell that lie.
Don't believe that lie.
Don't say hello.

Don't say goodbye.
Don't think that.
Don't want that.
Don't refuse that.
Don't hide.
Don't run away.
Don't cry.

And the flash goes off and another moment passes, perhaps another self-inflicted crack or a chip here and there, the dents of desperate and deliberate decisions. Trending toward empty, bordering on discarded, left in hope of redemption. Wondering at my worth.

> *You see, at just the right time, when we were still powerless, Christ died for the ungodly. Very rarely will anyone die for a righteous man, though for a good man someone might possibly dare to die. But God demonstrates His own love for us in this: While we were still sinners, Christ died for us. -- Romans 5:6-8*

I am valuable, not because of myself, but because God chose to love me. I am so redeemed.

But what of this trail of sin, so easily traced? Regardless of the reasons we sin, we sin. Yes, I was abandoned by my father, sexually-abused as a boy, a wandering and needy easy target for fellow sexual sinners. But, the scarlet sins that grew from this fertile soil were tended by my own hand. The regret and the remorse are the fruits of my own weakness.

> *Watch and pray so that you will not fall into temptation. The spirit is willing, but the body is weak. -- Mark 14:38*

Too little watching, too little praying, way too much falling. I'm responsible.

But, regret and remorse can morph into redeemed and restored in the hands of a God who does more than trace that trail. He sweeps it clean. He establishes a new trail. And He walks it with us.

No, He runs. If we run.

> *Therefore, since we have so great a cloud of witnesses surrounding us, let us also lay aside every encumbrance and the sin which so easily entangles us, and let us run with endurance the race that is set before us, fixing our eyes on Jesus, the author and perfecter of faith, who for the joy set before Him endured the cross, despising the shame, and has*

sat down at the right hand of the throne of God. For consider Him who has endured such hostility by sinners against Himself, so that you will not grow weary and lose heart. -- Hebrews 12:1-3

Believe me . . . witnesses surround me, not just the saints that came before. And there are encumbrances and sins. And they have entangled. But . . . God says to lay those things aside. God says to run with endurance, which means it was never going to be easy. God says to fix our eyes on Jesus, which means we should ignore the tempting scenery that flashes by as we head for the finish line.

I am sorry that Jesus endured my shame and I am in awe that He did so despite the fact He despised it. He endured it . . . so I could also. So that I would not grow weary. So I would not lose heart.

So I can finish.

And He provides help, in the form of fellow runners who help set the pace and in the form of those who cheer the progress of those who run.

One of my favorite camera views of televised marathons are of the outstretched hands along the way that hold forth a paper cup of water. The runner grabs it almost without pause, gulps it down, drops the cup on the road and keeps running. Even saying thanks at that point consumes too much energy, so the appreciation is silence and a renewed stamina to finish the race. Still, the person on the sidelines cheers and knows he helped provide the endurance.

Sometimes we are the runner, wondering how much further we have to go before we can collapse on the ground and breathe deeply of the clarity of completion.

Sometimes we are the one who stands and offers a taste of the living water that rushes through and replenishes the rebellious body. Either way, we are in this together . . . and we can finish well. If we don't lose heart. If we do not grow weary.

Sadly, some people in our lives will choose to be stumbling-blocks rather than water-bearers. If we fix our eyes on Jesus, He will help us jump those hurdles. We will all come to the end of the race at some point. Which face will we wear? One of regret or one of restoration?

We are all so valuable. We are so redeemed.

Don't stop.

The finish line is marked with the tape of grace.

CHAPTER 2

WHERE WOULD WE BE
WITHOUT DOUBT?

Lord, I crawled across the barrenness to you with my empty cup
uncertain in asking for any small drop of refreshment.
If only I had known you better, I'd have come running with a bucket.
--- *Nancy Spielberg*

One of the hardest things anyone with a significant struggle -- such as same-sex attraction, lust or pornography addiction -- deals with, is doubt. Self-doubt, sure. But, also the doubt others have in his or her ability to change . . . or even doubt that the person really wants to change. Sometimes this doubt is not truly expressed, but is instead hidden behind the "we're with you" smiles, which can so quickly become "we knew it" frowns at the very first sign of a fall. How nice it would be for all involved if this battle were but a minor skirmish with a certain outcome, instead of one of those "well, I had my doubts all along" battlefields, littered with the wounded, some doubting they can get themselves back up again to move forward, some doubting if anyone even cares anymore.

I had a friend in college who seemed to live with no doubts. He was always sure his project would be the best. He would sing the song just fine. His parents would, of course, send the money. His car would run. His jokes would always be funny and people would laugh. He would always be understood. His friends would ever be loyal and everything would complete itself perfectly, right on time. He was never timid or understated because he never doubted. But, he was also pretty much tied up in secret knots of frustration. He'd exchanged doubt for denial. When he didn't win first place or his joke fell flat or the check didn't arrive or the tire went flat or a friend let him down, he would bottle up inside and close down. What most of us might have lived through as dashed hope, he died to as devastation. His forced-open eyes would fill with tears of anguish. He definitely needed some doubt.

I haven't seen him in many years, but I "doubt" he is as certain of everything as he used to be.

Some might say my friend had faith. But the presence of faith is not the absence of doubt. Faith is based on a belief in hope. It involves assurance . . . and trust. This friend lived on assumption, not assurance. A little too much "it'll be all right," and a little too little "what will be will be." He had no faith to test because he allowed no doubt.

But what if we have a lot of doubt? Does that mean we have little faith?

I remember I used to sit on the curb in front of our house on Saturdays when I was a little boy. I doubted my dad would show, but I had faith that he would. Could the measure of each -- doubt or faith -- be determined by how long I sat with my chin on my knees looking to the left and right to see if he might come walking up the street?

I have no doubt God clearly knows the difference between doubt and faith. I'm not sure we always do. On our own, we usually reward our doubt with our deepest fears. Our faith, on the other hand, is usually God-tested and leads us to our greatest joy. "A little while" of testing can feel like a long time . . . and produce an awful lot of doubt.

> *In this you greatly rejoice, though now for a little while you may have had to suffer grief in all kinds of trials. These have come so that your faith -- of greater worth than gold, which perishes even though refined by fire -- may be proved genuine and may result in praise, glory and honor when Jesus Christ is revealed. -- I Peter 1:6-7*

It used to bother me that, of all the Biblical characters, I was named Thomas. The doubter. I know my mother did not really name me Thomas because she was debating which biblical character I would be like. After all, my brother's name is Mike, and my sisters' names are Deb and Sue. Mother was merely reflecting the popular name choices of the decade in which we were born. We could have as easily been Bob and Gary and Judy and Peggy. But I was Thomas, the doubter.

I think God loves those who doubt. In dealing with our sincere doubt, He demonstrates the truth that He is patient and kind. It is a wonderful truth that the greatest doubters often become the greatest believers. Our honest doubts can become the bedrock of our faith. Truth that comes rampaging in to dispel doubt is sweet and strong.

Maybe we should think less about what doubt is . . . and less about who doubts us . . . and instead think about what doubt may do. How does it motivate us? Does our doubt send us searching, or hiding? Revealing or masking?

Doubt is like looking out the window and seeing the sun go down for the gazillionth time, knowing once again that the darkness will follow, mimicking the darkness inside us. We might forget momentarily that the sun is only gone for a while. It does not yield its place to darkness in God's creative balance. Through grace, the light comes back around to overwhelm the darkness . . . lest anyone doubt. We strive hard to resist letting our sexual sin define us; let's not let our doubt do it either. You've read the Bible. Yes, people wander, but they are never beyond the gaze of God.

But what of those who doubt us or the sincerity of our quest for freedom? I say, let each doubter bear his own. Sometimes we expend so much energy trying to dispel the doubts of others that we have too little energy left to put on the armor for our own battles. Let them doubt. God can deal with that. And, if they want someday to put their hands in your scars, scarcely believing this new you is . . . you . . . then let them do so and forgive their doubt as you forgive your own.

Some may tell us we've used up all our chances. They've moved beyond doubting to knowing. "You *can't* change." Well . . . life is not a game of chance; it is a reality of faith. Let them keep their assumption; you have your assurance.

I am thankful for doubt. Anyone who struggles with temptation knows that doubt is a glimpse of freedom. If we can doubt, we can seek.

Doubt leads us to the door. That door where you knock. Where you ask. That door that opens. Behind which no despair lingers. Where doubt no longer dwells.

Ask and it will be given to you; seek and you will find; knock and the door will be opened to you. For everyone who asks receives; he who seeks finds; and to him who knocks, the door will be opened. -- Matthew 7: 7-8

And if for some unfounded reason you doubt that the word "everyone" includes you, then let *that* doubt lead you to the door. It will open . . . no doubt.

CHAPTER 3

PLUGGING THE LEAK
IN THE LIFEBOAT

Sometimes we can become so attached to the familiarity of life -- the good and the bad -- that we become far too comfortable, whether we are wallowing or jubilating. Snug in our surroundings and safe in our stability or even in our instability, we become satisfied that at least it is us. Black or white, wrong or right, the reflection in the mirror, smiling or frowning, singing or crying, is me.

I have been asked why it is that I seem okay today, despite the harsh realities of reaping. I'm still separated from my children, some past church issues remain unsettled, my not-quite-completely-resolved mind stubbornly challenges my clearly-resolved soul for clarity and purpose. Add to that lack of clarity a blurred vision for my future as a provider and my place as a servant. But I'm okay. Or, to use that all-purpose Christian four-letter word: I'm *fine*.

My okayness is more than just going with the flow. At an early age, I thought life would never be all that good . . . and it has turned out far better than good, based on my internal measurements. Observers -- both the casual and the highly-critical -- may disagree, but experience tells me that the value of observation can be greatly affected by both distance and distortion.

I had low expectations from an early age and I stand amazed at the goodness of God despite what I expect or suspect. My perspective has changed through the life experience of the grading process, the piling up of tests; some failed, some passed. I have experienced the blessing of being graded on the curve.

When I was about 10, the *good* part of my life revolved around a couple of goofy friends, a bicycle with a banana seat and high-rise handlebars, and a place to ride it. The bad part of my life resided in a small drab apartment ruled by a stepfather who drank a lot of whiskey while lounging around in an old frayed robe, smoked a lot of cigarettes, shouted a lot of curse words and slept a lot of time away in front of the TV. Outside was the place to be, even if the great outdoors consisted mainly of miles of parking lots crammed between other drab apartment buildings stretching on for blocks.

Freedom could be found in the acres of land outside our Houston suburb that had been cleared for the building of a major expressway. The bulldozers had created mountains of dirt and we carved trails through them and raced each other up and down and around, flying faster each time because we were so familiar. We followed our own tracks. Our rubber tires were so "one-with-the-dirt," we could have flown through the dusty mountain trails hands-raised with blindfolds on.

Flying became more real one morning when I came to the end of the tallest "mountain" and found that the bulldozers which had given had begun the taketh away phase. The end of the mountain was gone; a cliff was there and I pedaled into the sky and the rubber became one with the air. It doesn't take long for a 10-year-old's life to flash before his eyes, even a life as muddled and odd as the one I had already lived.

I survived. A bit of blood, a bunch of bruises, a lot of bends in the bike. I realized that even the best-laid trails can turn against you.

A few years ago, on a cold winter night, I came home from teaching an evening writing class at the university. Lisa was out that evening and left a dinner in the fridge, which I warmed up. I carried it to the living room to watch "24." I took a bite, took a drink, took a bite, and took a drink. And then I panicked. Not one bite of food, not one swallow of iced tea had followed the trail -- the esophagus -- down to the eager stomach. I could not swallow at all. My mind -- which has never been very scientific -- deduced that if I could not swallow, I could not breathe. I just knew I was dying, sitting on a couch with a plate of uneaten leftovers, all alone on a cold night. I wouldn't even have time to leave a thank-you note behind.

Of course, we don't breathe through the esophagus. Our lungs are not attached to our stomachs. As soon as the now-extended life quit flashing before my eyes, I had to force myself to throw up, called my wife and then a doctor and the next day went in to have the esophagus dilated and opened up so I could eat again. I celebrated with a chocolate shake.

I survived.

Maybe we all need, once or twice, to face the reality of death, even if it is not really real reality, just a panic as the gap closes between us and the hard ground . . . or the mind confuses the anatomy and declares it's closing time.

One of the things I've learned is that my lack of trust in the Lord tended often to result in a transfer of trust to others. I think it's good to know people we can trust and believe in, but "In God We Trust" are not just four little words that started appearing on a two-cent coin in 1864 as a result of a minister's plea following the Civil War. "In God We Trust" are the words that will guide us through our own civil wars, when one side of us stands in opposition to the other and we threaten to tear ourselves apart.

We are a sea of strugglers. Who calmed the seas? So, in whom shall we trust? Obviously in the One who turns the raging sea of remorse into the enabling sea of forgetfulness. No one else can do it . . . and if we are looking for someone else . . . our lifeboat has a serious leak.

We don't need to carry the excess baggage of one year into the next. I want to travel lighter, be surer of foot, choose a better trail, and become one with the One. I grew so sick of stumbling in the past that I was gravely in danger of dropping all pretense of walking . . . and just about decided it was time to give up. But . . . we press on.

Brothers, I do not consider myself yet to have taken hold of it. But one thing I do: Forgetting what is behind and straining toward what is ahead, I press on toward the goal to win the prize for which God has called me heavenward in Christ Jesus. -- Philippians 3:13-14

Forgetting what is behind?
Straining toward what is ahead?
Pressing on toward the goal?
For which God has called . . . . me?
Trust God.
Not the trails I lay out for myself.
Not my body.
Not my mind.
Not people . . . though there are those placed in my life who are trust-merchants for the Lord.
Trust God.

The road to restoration will be cleared by removing the separation that remains between me and Him because of the sins I hold so dear. The familiarity of the life I choose has too-long veiled the adventure of the one to which He calls. I am moving from the valley of low expectations to the peaks of His promises.

Trust.

Trust God.

Mighty God.

CHAPTER 4

THE BULLY IN THE BARN

He is jealous for me.
Loves like a hurricane
I am a tree
Bending beneath the weight of His wind and mercy,
When all of a sudden
I am unaware of these
Afflictions eclipsed by glory.
And I realize just how beautiful you are and
How great Your affections are for me.

-- John Mark MacMillan

This is a story about a kid named Spike. He was, for me, a great affliction. I have asked for forgiveness for thinking of him as such, but I will never forget the "Summer of Spike."

Jonathan Edwards, preacher and missionary to Native Americans back in the 1700s, and widely acknowledged to be America's most important and original philosophical theologian and a great intellect, included affliction among his famous resolutions about how to live his life, which he wrote in 1723. There it was, number 67 out of 70:

Resolved, after afflictions, to inquire, what I am the better for them, what good I have got by them, and what I might have got by them.

Jonathan Edwards read his resolutions every week . . . as if afflictions need a reminder. If Jonathan Edwards had ever spent a summer with Spike, he would have never needed a refresher on affliction.

One encounter with Spike and you would never forget him, no matter how resolved you might be to do so. And though my encounter with him took place only over the span of perhaps three days, I call it the Summer of Spike because I really don't remember anything else about that summer. He was an impactful kind of kid.

The Summer of Spike might be more aptly remembered as the summer of shame. It followed a winter of abandonment and a spring of seduction. Winter being the season of my father's separation from my life and spring being the following season of sexual abuse at the hands of the evil one who presumed to take my father's place as my protector and mentor.

As I moved into that summer, I was a much-too-wise-eight-year-old and a bearer of secrets. Secrets deep within me were going through the metamorphosis that would convert them into scars.

Silence like a cancer grows? In me, it was more like silence like a cancer flows. I had turned into a bed-wetter. The shame I hid during my daytime interactions with "normal" people seeped out of me at night and multiplied. I would try not to drink. I would try not to sleep. I would have tried anything. None of it worked. The stain that had taken hold of my life, which I buried out of sight, would find its way out in the midst of a sad dream and show up in the morning as a stain on my sheets. It was just another reason to wish I had never been born.

I would soon wish someone else had never been born.

My new stepfather's parents lived on a farm near Stroud, Oklahoma. It was picturesque. A fading red barn with implements and tractors all around, big horses and rowdy cows, bins full of cornstalks, a sawdust floor, an owl in the rafters, ropes hanging from the beams for uses I couldn't imagine, a rooster in the second-floor window, a weather vane on the peak. And a sorta' cousin named Spike, whose parents -- for some odd reason -- had sent him there to spend the summer with his grandparents.

I never caught my step-grandparents' names and knew them only as "Mom" and "Dad," which is what my stepfather called them. I caught my cousin's name right off. I'd never known a Spike and I wonder now how his parents could have been so prophetic in naming their child.

I was a skinny little eight-year-old bed-wetter in the hands of a twelve-year-old bully pursuing perfection for his chosen calling. I wasted no time inviting affliction upon myself. Spike was a farm boy, and by the end of the first night I was so exhausted from all the things he had done to me trying to turn me into his little farmhand, that I fell fast asleep . . . *deeply* asleep . . . in the same bed as Spike. He woke up yellowed and yelling.

"Mom" chased me into the hallway bathroom where I ended up standing naked in an old claw-footed bathtub while she poured cold water on me and pronounced me as lazy and stupid. Spike stood outside the open door pointing and laughing.

It gets worse.

The original plan had not been for me to stay at the farm that day when we had visited, but Spike had begged and my mother relented and left me there . . . with only the clothes I had on, which were also the clothes I had later slept in. My clothes were now in the wash and I was stuck wearing a pair of Spike's shorts. He was not a little 12-year-old by any stretch and my legs looked like they were extending from dual parachutes as we headed to the barn to feed the horses and play in the hay in the rafters.

About halfway up the ladder, I heard Spike's laughter and looked down to see him pointing. He could see up my -- well, his -- shorts and was ridiculing me in a way that an experience-damaged little boy can't just accept as teasing. It was torment and torture. Spike had already wrestled me into surrender on a dusty floor, thrown me into a near-stagnant stock pond, bludgeoned me with a pillow, offered me as a human sacrifice to a bunch of hungry cows and mocked me in a bathtub.

I heard years later that Spike dived into a shallow swimming pool later that summer while showing off and cracked his burred head. I never saw him again, but heard he had survived, yet would always have a nasty and permanent scar. So did I.

Even after we survive our childhood, I think there are times when we just give in and see ourselves as others sometimes see us, as less than them, as somehow not put together quite right, as willingly astray, pleasurably-broken, struggle-embracing, skinny little creatures paralyzed on a ladder, ridiculed and diminished and deserving to be so.

We need instead to see ourselves as Jesus sees us. Jesus see us as complete. He doesn't toss us into stock ponds; He picks us up and wraps us in His arms and simply loves us. He doesn't wrestle us into forced surrender; He *invites* us to surrender and soothes us with grace and peace. He doesn't point and mock, reducing us to shame; He holds and hears and builds us back up with hope.

Jesus doesn't exploit our weaknesses. When we're weak; He is strong. He never makes us wish we had never been born; he makes us rejoice to be born again.

I wish all the afflictions which serve as such fertile soil for the morphing of experiences into the scars that so taunt strugglers could vanish into the night like the hoots of the old barn owl that no longer haunt me. Rather than manifesting themselves into such burdens, I wish these afflictions could be as distant a memory for you as Spike is now for me.

But . . . what of Jonathan Edwards and his resolution that such afflictions are to be turned into good? And, what about the Old Testament's Joseph, sold into slavery by his very brothers? That was certainly worse than being roughed up in a hay barn by a crazy cousin.

> *You intended to harm me, but God intended it all for good. He brought me to this position so I could save the lives of many people.—Genesis 50:20*

Joseph had a very positive perspective, considering what he had been through. I know it is tough to "count it all joy." I know it is hard to see how God can intend it all for good. But if we allow ourselves to be trapped inside the vision that others have created for us and wear the label they have fashioned for us, and limit ourselves to their diminished hope, we empower Satan. If we trust God and take Him at His word and obey Him and surrender and find our hope in Glory, we confound Satan.

Our afflictions *are* eclipsed by Glory. Our earthly afflictions are no match for His heavenly affections. *Oh . . . how He loves us.*

I rarely think of Spike. He's probably a kindly grandfather somewhere. Maybe when he sees "shortcomings" in his grandchildren he thinks of his "Summer of Thom" and cuts them a little slack. He usually only comes to my mind when a sportscaster notes the futility that leads a quarterback to "spike" the ball. I always think of Spike diving into that pool.

Be strong.

Be courageous.

Be obedient.

And when you find yourself being less than what God intends and trapped somewhere in what man pretends, remember how much He loves you. Vanquish the bully in the barn and walk with the One who really knows you.

CHAPTER 5

QUIET HOPE . . . OR BITTER RESIGNATION?

And the God of all grace, who called you to His eternal glory in Christ, after you have suffered a little while, will Himself restore you and make you strong, firm and steadfast. -- 1 Peter 5:10

Wouldn't it be nice if emotions and feelings came with labels, like green beans and cookies? We could just scan the can or peruse the package and know whether this was going to be good for us or make us blow up like a balloon. Or, how about a label to tell us where they came from, like "Made in China?" The label might read, "Fashioned in a Deceitful Heart," or "Dredged up from Dependency." Maybe a warning label would be nice: "Warning: Acting on this Feeling May Cause User to Spiral Out of Control," or "Beware: This Emotion May Be Hazardous to Personal Stability." Since so many feelings can be toxic, maybe the warning labels could contain antidotes: turn, pray, flee.

But, for the person who struggles with sexual brokenness, life is not always nice and it is certainly not packaged for ease of opening. Nor do all the pieces seem to easily go together, if they're even all there. So we decorate the packages and overlook the missing and broken pieces and do our best to assemble the best life we can with whatever went into our basket at checkout. Sometimes it shows; sometimes it doesn't. It depends on our marketing skills and how well we sell ourselves to others . . . and to ourselves. We know "the truth is out there," but we prefer to be in here. We curl up with a little of the truth like a too-small blanket and want for greater comfort and security.

Is it "quiet hope" or "bitter resignation?" Is it waiting or wilting? When rains come, do they wash us clean and set our feet to freedom or could they be the final flood that grows ever deeper to sweep us away?

I remember a little girl who lived down the street from me in a small town when I was a boy. In my fractured and unpredictable world, a good day was defined as a day that nothing bad happened. I looked forward to those. In her little world though, only a few blocks away, a day was defined as good. Her daddy was determined she know no bad.

We lived in the tornado belt and spring storms ranged from frequent to constant. The dark clouds would come flying over the horizon, billowing miles high, filled with the flashes of lightning, thunder echoing throughout the sky. Birds would flee and dogs would cower as the clouds organized into dangerous whirlwinds, sizing up targets and we would hide in bathtubs under rugs. Soon, the sun would come out and the wet trees would glisten in amazing brilliance and we would ride our bikes in the tiny rivers along the curbs. That was how life was: powerful and menacing one moment; peaceful and contrite the next. Just like at home: blow up and tear up, then make up and clean up.

The daddy of the little girl down the lane had a curious habit of making sure that everything bad turned out good. After every storm, when the thunder ceased and the lightning faded, he would sneak out into their backyard and hang candy on the tree that grew in the center of the yard, just behind his daughter's bedroom. She never saw him do it, but would see the candy dangling like magic outside her window and run out to get it and forget there had ever been a storm in the first place. He assured her there never would be, not really.

Our trees were always candy-bare after the storms, surrounded by a few broken branches and loosened leaves, but I would usually slip down the street to the little girl's house to see if the candy had appeared. I knew it was just her dad that hung it there, but I wanted to think that somehow God was doing it.

Of course, I've learned since then that sometimes the storm itself is the "candy," or at least the consequence. It's the result of all the build up, the choices, the things we ignore, the wants we confuse with the needs, the piled-up discarded warning labels, the substituted ingredients, the parts we twisted in hopes they would fit. Finally, a little thunder, a flash of lightning, a growing swirling and the birds are fleeing and the dogs are cowering . . . and so are we, beneath the weight of our own heaviness, searching in vain for that little soft blanket of truth we used to pull over our heads before we weaved a bigger and expanding replacement from the fabric of false hope. And then . . . thar she blows.

And our tears are like rain. And they overflow. And in our cowardly confusion, knowing we allowed this toxic storm into our lives, we ignore the antidote: turn, pray, flee. Indeed, many times we seek comfort in the darkness of the cloud itself and stir it to a greater intensity.

Praise be to the God and Father of our Lord Jesus Christ, the Father of compassion and the God of all comfort, who comforts us in all our troubles, so that we can comfort those in any trouble with the comfort we ourselves have received from God. For just as the sufferings of Christ flow over into our lives, so also through Christ our comfort overflows. -- 2 Corinthians 1:3-5

We can trade our cowardly confusion for the compassion and comfort of Christ.

Come to me, all you who are weary and burdened, and I will give you rest. -- Matthew 11:28

Come?
All?
Weary?
Burdened?
Rest?

Really then, what are our excuses for holding on and holding in those burdens that make us so weary that we perfect our storm-creation skills and run for cover when the actions of our hands and hearts grow into chaos? Aren't we among the "all?" Wouldn't we rather "rest?" In Him?

I think sometimes we get so busy counting the costs that we forget to rejoice in the gains. For one, we've not been swept away, we've been swept up. We've not been given the dead limp limbs from a storm-tossed weeping willow, but the sweet fruits of grace and mercy dangling deliciously from a strong and mighty tree. We're not tossed about and discarded; we're lifted up and swept high.

Don't think I am putting my head in the clouds and dismissing the damages. I hurt. You hurt. Struggling does that. It takes a portion of us and puts it in opposition to the rest of us, so we feel the pulling until it seems we might just come apart. And then, behold, the One who knit us together in our mothers' wombs offers to restore and redeem and repair.

If we hope.

If we do not succumb to the bitterness of resignation.

If we can look just above the heap of loss to the horizon of hope.

My sins have cost me the respect of my children, the security of my former career, the respect of those who saw the candy but missed the brittle branches of deception on which it hung and turned away, repelled at the revelation. But, in all these things I have hope. I am not resigned.

Why?

The storms that erupt don't just tear away the good, they wash away the bad. The just and the unjust. So much decaying debris has now been swept away it was like a rushing flood crashing through a logjam. Perhaps when our lives get so filled with crud, there is nothing we can do but experience a flood to allow for removal and replacing. A flood of repentance.

I know a lot of people are just trying to hold on. Struggling with sexual brokenness is a form of suffering that often seems deserved not only in the eyes of our observers, but in our own. Why are we so weak? Inquiring minds really . . . really . . . *really* want to know.

We should be asking ourselves why we are so hesitant to ask the Strong Deliverer, the One who never grows weary, never faints, defends the weak, comforts, gives us hope, and offers to lift us up on wings like eagles, to do it. He will outlast every storm.

So, where are you today? Reaching high in quiet hope? Bent low in bitter resignation? I know your hurt is real. Those storms are not imaginary. And no one runs around behind them hanging treats to make your fear subside. I know the hope is real too. And the reward of our hope is forgiveness, redemption, truth and love and freedom.

The reward of resignation is . . . . bitterness. And inaction. We become stumps, perhaps impervious to the pounding of the storms, but resistant to the sun as well. We stop growing.

Maybe you're somewhere in the middle, a little short of hope, just skirting the border of bitterness. Often it is when we are muddled in the middle that we discover the clarity of grace to drive us in the better direction.

> *Therefore, since we have been justified through **faith**, we have **peace** with God through our Lord Jesus Christ, through whom we have gained access by faith into this **grace** in which we now stand. And we rejoice in the **hope** of the **glory** of God. Not only so, but we also rejoice in our sufferings, because we know that suffering produces **perseverance**. -- Romans 5:1-3*

There's the reward: faith . . . peace . . . grace . . . hope . . . perseverance. And there's the choice: rejoice in our sufferings and persevere or resign to them and drown in bitterness.

Be resolved to rejoice.

CHAPTER 6

IN THE COMFORT OF
THE CLEARING

*O taste and see that the Lord is good; how blessed is the
man who takes refuge in Him! -- Psalm 34:8*

*The Lord is near to the brokenhearted and saves those
who are crushed in spirit. -- Psalm 34:18*

A small part of me wants to hang on to vengeance. I find myself looking
back and wishing I could repay some harms, teach a few lessons here and
there, put one or two folks in their places (wherever that would be) and
perhaps point a few fingers of righteousness at ones I declare wicked. But,
there is a larger part of me that is thankful that vengeance is the Lord's.
There's another part of me that also wishes everyone else knew and believed
that -- *that vengeance is the Lord's* -- and would quit trying to do what
God has said He will take care of. So, you see, I have many parts, being
"wondrously made." No wonder God's love has to be so deep and wide.
I'm so often veering one way or another, up or down, side-to-side.

Still, His mercy is just inescapable. Vengeance? Maybe also?

In my life, mercy often appears like a clearing in the woods. At just
the point where it seems that one more thorny vine or scratching tangled
brush, or one more exhaustive lost step of wandering would be too much,
a clearing appears with a view from ground to sky and I am reminded that
even when the path appears overgrown and treacherous, threatening to
swallow me up in dangerous darkness, there is a clearing. Room to breathe,
to rest, to wait, to renew my strength, to ponder past missteps and consider
a new course before pushing forward. Mercy.

Even in my darkest moments of being abused, or my black times of determined depravity, or when frittering here and there in the shadows of sexual brokenness, or slinking along in the gray dealing of dishonesty, there were clearings, those points where I felt clearly the presence of God. Sometimes I would behave like a possum caught in a sudden light and curl up in defense, playing dead and waiting for the moment to move beyond me. Other times I would flee, fur-flying like a fox caught in the barn of iniquity by a bright and frightening light, and run into the darkness to hide and plan another deceitful descent. Other times I would throw my hands in the air in a "you caught me" moment of surrender. Mostly I would sit still and silent to consider carefully the consequences of letting my tears flow and my heart open as opposed to the consequences of fighting back the tears, burying the heart deeper and moving forward on my own with steely determination. Oh, the choices we make when the light shines in dark places.

It seems strange to me that so many of the worst things in life happen within the most beautiful circumstances. My final abusive moment in the hands of a sexually-deviant Scout master came when I was around 8. He knew a place just outside of town that was like heaven for little boys. A short distance from the railroad tracks, next to a flowing stream which fed a bright blue and clear pond surrounded by polished stones on which turtles sunned. It was just a short hike, punctuated by stopping to collect a few loose railroad spikes, skip some rocks on the pond and then settle down in the sun. I have never forgotten the beauty of the place and have often wanted to find it again, but I have a feeling a housing addition sits there now, happy little homes built around the peaceful pond that was once my clearing. I was not even a Christian at that age, yet I clearly remember standing on the banks and seeing my reflection there and believing I was not alone. The water was bright and beautiful and I did not play possum, but instead took strength from that believing.

God has always provided these places of clarity at times when it seems I would be driven deaf by the clanging callousness of life, or permanently disabled by my own clanging gongs and cymbals. How many times I stood upon the edge of a cliff, lifted a foot and prepared to step into thin air, only to be distracted by immeasurable love.

My sheep listen to My voice; I know them, and they follow Me. -- John 10:27

And I would turn.

If only I had been able to always distinguish His voice from among the cacophony crying out. Why was I such a frequent visitor to the edge? Was it to test His faithfulness? Perhaps I want to know for sure that as unlovely as I am, God does indeed love me. And how He has proved it over and over.

What about you? *I know.* One day not so long ago you were sure . . . and then a few forays into darkness later . . . the surety seems dimmed, clouded by layers of sinful residue.

> *Repent, then, and turn to God, so that your* **sins** *may be* **wiped out,** *that times of* **refreshing** *may come from the Lord.* -- Acts 3:19

I look for the approval of men in my sin . . . and then I seek the approval of men when I stop. Yet, only God really knows my heart and only God knows what it will take to refresh it. So, it is when I set men aside in good times and bad and put God first that I gain from my time in the clearing and it becomes more than a passing place of pause and reflection.

I know some of the people reading this were moments ago perhaps surfing the web for porn, or fighting off the urge to enter a cycle of sexual fantasy, or feeling the pull to step outside the bonds of a God-ordained marriage to find self-centered satisfaction. And I know some feel entitled, longing for a way to bury deeper the scars of the distant past, or to escape the pain of a difficult present. Some are in pain, some are in denial, some are in a desperate cycle fueled by a displaced sense of unworthiness. This is not a happy path. But . . . there is a clearing.

When we recognize we are sinful and tend to take the wrong path.

When we realize that our sinfulness is a rebellion against the very God that has cleared our path.

When we admit we know all this and resign ourselves to helplessness, admitting we have been lost and stumbling, ignoring our guide.

When we trust in God's willingness to forgive and again shine the light for our feet to follow.

When we actually accept His forgiveness and take His hand to lead us out of the darkness.

When we stand in the clearing, look around us at the underbrush and tangled clutter from which we have been rescued.

When we stop and look up, surrounded by threatening but held-back darkness and observe the brightness of the night sky and the sweet comfort of the approaching dawn.

When we know we are not alone.

When?

We stumble along way too long.

The unsettling thing about a clearing is that the clutter that surrounds often still remains. In my case, that includes the former friends and church-members who are overwhelmed by skepticism and shuttered. Or my children who decided I delved in that darkness too long and am the mole in the hole instead of the bird in flight. Still, the sense of peace that clearly passes understanding is the prize we receive when we pause in the clearing and accept His loving-kindness. I'll take the peace; perhaps the understanding may one day follow.

If God can restore me, once deemed unworthy among unworthies -- and He has -- I can certainly trust Him to restore all worthy things.

And I can wait. Here . . . in the clearing.

CHAPTER 7

WALKING DOWN THE ROAD OF LIFE

In the stillness of the night and the darkness of my room,
A tear teased at the corner of my eye.
At the window through the curtains and beneath the silent moon
I once again addressed Him with my why?

In the brightness of the day in my room I sat and stared,
Broken, I allowed myself to cry.
But the window in my mind said despite it all He cared
So I once again addressed Him with my why?

He's so patient, so forbearing, yet in His truth unyielding,
And He doesn't turn away when I ask why.
Though it's often in His silence that He does His truth revealing
As He quietly continues by my side.
Are you broken? Let Me see.
He looked deep into my eyes.
I could feel that God was moving
And I knew He heard my cries.

-- Thom Hunter

Life is full of firsts. First steps. First lost tooth. First birthday. First day at school. First car. First love. Somewhere in there is a first fall. We might not have seen it, but it happened. It probably felt more like a compromise than a fall, but it was a tumble nonetheless and -- at least for the moment -- it stretched the distance between ourselves and the hand of God. We might not even have noticed the separation. If we had, we would have scrambled back like a toddler when he suddenly rebels against the freedom he so wanted and runs back into the outstretched arms. Restored to safety. It is well.

I don't remember my first steps, tooth, birthday, day at school. I do remember my first car and I remember a first love, though the closest I came to her was kissing her through a screen door on her front porch. I ran as fast as I could and never approached that porch again. I've forgotten her name now; I was only about 10. Some firsts definitely deserve to fade.

I also remember my first car. It was a 1960 Ford Falcon, bright red and purchased for $300, paid out at $25 a month. I was 15. In that first car, I discovered my first clutch. It never occurred to me when my boss dropped me off at the used car lot and drove away, that the car I had chosen -- based strictly on price -- was not an automatic like my mother's pink Buick. I had no idea how to drive it, and if I could have driven it all the way home in first gear, I would have. Even better, if someone had pulled up next to me and asked me to give it away to them, I would have.

What I really needed, as I struggled to cross town in a car with an unforgiving standard transmission and a very hard clutch was for someone to pull up beside me and say "do you need some help there, young man?" No honking horns or pointing fingers, no snickering, no rolling eyes. Just a little help, please.

I had never been that flustered and frustrated and I had never so deeply failed. But I ground on home and, once it was in the driveway, the car shifted from "stupid" to "stupendous."

Which leads me to the first fall. This is not the tumble-into-a-coffee-table-while-learning-to-walk type fall. No, I'm talking about a pre-meditated, pre-determined, pre-weighed, definitely-decided-upon headlong tumble into pit-like darkness. A pre-acknowledged clear and present "I'm sinning" moment. Not the "we're all born in sin" reality, but the reality that I, fully aware, totally conscious, of clear mind, chose to sin. Knew it; did it. Took a tiptoe into the winking wilderness that winds its way alongside the path to the abundant life. A daring and defiant detour into the shadows.

Confessed and forgiven, I can spare you the details. Disappointed? Don't be. First falls are generally messy affairs; we brush ourselves off and look over the bruises and make vows. It takes a little practice to perfect our pursuit of sin, just as it does our pursuit of holiness. The two pursuits are often intermingled and can leave us famished in a land of plenty.

If we are not careful, we can confuse our detour with our destination. We can forget where we were headed in the first place when we took an off-ramp and rambled around in the hinterlands, avoiding for a bit the hithertoos. We need a good wake-up call in the form of a correcting come hither so we can we get back on the right road again and chart a course where the broken find abundance.

The devil is not just in the details; he's out on the detour, ready to strip the hubcaps off, tossing nails in the roadway. For the sexually-broken, he's lurking like a hitchhiker flashing whatever it takes to reel you off to the side of the road. Men and women addicted to pornography find free showings at the detour rest stop. For the men and women who struggle with unwanted same-sex attractions he throws up seductive messages on the detour's billboards to take you further and further out of your way. For the lonely, he lowers the lights along the way to make life seem ever greyer and he closes the detour coffee shop just as you pull into the parking lot to make you ever more lonely and needy. He knows how to make you stray.

The thief comes only to steal and kill and destroy; I came that they may have life, and have it abundantly. -- John 10:10

The devil sometimes has some strange accomplices, most of them unaware of how he uses them to complicate our finding our way back on track. These are the ones who, well meaning or not, cause us to shift our focus off of Christ and onto them. Making us performers on a perfection path, they hold out rewards of righteousness if we can but prove our repentance to the point of relieving all their reservations about us. Christians can be so . . . un-Christian. Our pursuit of holiness can become a pursuit of approval: a detour.

I remember when I was past my darkest point of having been revealed as a double-minded sinner drowning in waves of uncontrolled temptation to act out in sexual sin. Having been through the fire of accusations and having run the gauntlet of public embarrassment, I was like a battered boat against the boulders of the jagged coast, barely holding together under the relentless waves of earned judgment. I was ready for restoration; determined to repent; thirsting for reconciliation. They were poised for a performance, a display of some sort that would satisfy their repentance-restoration checklist.

"You're not broken," they told me.

I could barely hear them, as my ears were worn from the accusations I had to hear repeated against me before my confession, still ringing from the recantation of my sinful reveling.

"I'm not what?"

"You're not broken."

"You can tell me that?" I thought, looking at the pieces of me lying around the room. "What does broken look like to you, if this is not broken?"

"We'll know it when we see it."

They never have. And maybe never will. It is unlikely I will do the brokenness approval dance, which is probably just as dangerous as the other disastrous dances we do throughout our lives for the approval of others, the price we pay here and there to open a door or gain access or achieve an image. Do you like me now? Do we really want forgiveness if it has to be earned and bestowed upon us like a title in a talent show? Detours.

I guess it really depends on where we want to go.

Jesus said to him, "I am the way, and the truth, and the life; no one comes to the Father but through Me. -- John 14:6.

That's the no-detour route. It doesn't meander through the why wilderness or the valley of confusion or the depths of deceit. It's just truth. And life. And it isn't exclusionary. You don't fill out an application and go through an interview with the local approval committee to get a stamp of approval and a limited-use ticket. It's "the" way. He doesn't say there is anyone who cannot come; He just says there's only one way to get there. Just Him.

What I have discovered by trashing all the frequent-flyer miles earned by trying to prove myself pure enough for the approval of man is that the journey is lightened by the Light.

I have come as light into the world, so that everyone who believes in Me will not remain in darkness. -- John 12:46.

I know the dark; I love the light. Sometimes we arrive at abundance through the great cost of loss. And yet, we can count it all joy. I wish I had never wandered, but I am more conscious now than ever before at how determined He was to find me . . . even at the cost of His own life. He brought the dead back to life; He can direct the wayward out of a detour.

Suppose one of you has a hundred sheep and loses one of them. Does he not leave the ninety-nine in the open country and go after the lost sheep until he finds it? And when he finds it, he joyfully puts it on his shoulders and goes home. Then he calls his friends and neighbors together and says, 'Rejoice with me; I have found my lost sheep.' -- Luke 15:4-6

That's me. A sheep who, rather than be tended, tended to detour. And that's Him . . . a Shepherd who does not give up on His own. Who doesn't stand at arm's length and say "show me something," but instead picks me up, puts me across His shoulder and . . . *rejoices*. Wow . . . it's enough to deter you from detouring.

Wherever you've been . . . wherever you are . . . there is a place for you in the Kingdom of God. You won't have to prove your brokenness; He already knows.

CHAPTER 8

HIDING'S SUCH A LONELY THING TO DO

The game, as we all know, is called "Hide and Seek." While one player -- maybe your dad -- leans against a tree with his eyes closed and counts to 10, your friends -- your brothers and sisters -- go hide themselves behind the fences, up in the trees, under a parked car in the driveway, behind a bush. And then, when he is done counting, he seeks. In your quietness, you try to sneak past him and run back "home" without being caught.

The game, as we all know, is called "Life."

Sometimes we hide. Sometimes we seek. Sometimes we struggle desperately to make it back home unnoticed. Sometimes we hide beyond the established borders and perhaps just wander on as darkness falls and the seeker calls out our name . . . along with "All in . . . All in . . . all come free." And the seeker waits beside the tree, eyes open, expecting all. He knows our name and cups his hands and calls out into the darkness. And on we hide.

If God is the seeker, He waits. People, on the other hand, may move on. There will be other games in other places with other players. In either case, whether you are hiding from God or hiding from people, or perhaps even hiding from yourself . . . hiding is a very lonely thing to do.

When my children were little, they would hide in plain sight, or, at the least, in plain sound. Once, one of them covered his eyes and pronounced that since he could not see me, I could not see him. I think sometimes we approach God that way. We cover our eyes and take a little time out, as if He can not see us because we choose not to see Him.

Other times, one of my little ones would dash behind the nearest big chair and giggle and wiggle. Invisible but so uncontrollably happy at the prospect of being found that he would leave a vocal road map. The joy was not in the hiding, but in the being sought. We do that to God too; we make intentional noises and pray that He will follow them and pull us from the shadows of the big chair and sweep us up like He is surprised and overjoyed. And He does.

But sometimes we duck and turn and weave and wander to points where we don't even know where we are. And then we dig so deep that it is like we want to make sure our cries are muffled. We're not so sure we want to be found. It's not that we think He can't. We just kind of like it out here in the darker places.

When I would find my children in their favorite spots after walking around a bit and pretending not to see them, perhaps even giving them a chance to run full-speed to "home," I would catch them. And, what would they say? "Let's do it again, Daddy!" They wanted "do-overs."

And we would. Again and again. Hider and seeker, trading places on occasion. My turn to giggle and wiggle and be caught running home.

Of course, they're all grown now and their hiding and seeking is between them and their Maker, as all Christians discover. They Adam-and-Eve themselves into and out of His presence. And, they, like me, most likely plead for their share of do-overs, which come in the form of forgiveness, God's response to confession and repentance.

I'm not a great cook, being fortunate to be married to one. I like to make a few things, divinity being one of those. A couple of times a year I break out the Karo, beat up the egg whites and make the purest, whitest, dissolve-in-your-mouth candy. Or not. Much as I watch the candy thermometer to the exact degree, beat the egg whites to the stiffest and combine all the ingredients "slowly while beating," the divinity sometimes turns in to a sticky mess or a hard chalky unappealing brick.

Because everyone thinks I make "perfect" divinity, I just do a do-over. I dump out the inferior stuff and keep at it until it's as close to perfect as it can be. And no one sees the messes and the failures.

God wants perfection too. He didn't create us to be sticky-gooey or hard and chalky. We were intended to be a delight to all His senses. The recipe itself is perfect, but it seems to take a lot of doing-over to get it right. In God's kitchen, that means a purifying process, a washing.

Purify me with hyssop, and I shall be clean; wash me, and I shall be whiter than snow. -- Psalm 51:7

And it requires a lot of "Do-it-again-Daddy."

That is, if we don't just hide ourselves, which is certainly the first inclination when we have embarrassed ourselves and sinned again, perhaps, as has been said of me "against all of humanity."

I acknowledged my sin to You, And my iniquity I did not hide; I said, "I will confess my transgressions to the Lord," and You forgave the guilt of my sin. -- Psalm 32:5

King David learned a lot from hiding. What he learned most was to not do it anymore.

We have a God who does not wander; does not turn a deaf ear; does not flinch. He doesn't hide. In fact, He surrounds us with His presence, which makes seeking Him simply simple. To not seek Him, we have to want to not seek Him. We have to deny Him.

And without faith it is impossible to please God, because anyone who comes to Him must believe that He exists and that He rewards those who earnestly seek Him. -- Hebrews 11:6

But what if we are so discouraged that we have piled the darkness high around us like angry black stones to block all vision and progress? He turns the table and He does the seeking.

For the Son of Man has come to seek and to save that which was lost. -- Luke 19:10

So what is a sinner to do? We live in a world that acknowledges sin all the time. We talk about it. Report on it. Point at it. Rebuke it. Judge it. Mimic it. Teach it. Punish it. Enjoy it. Drown in it. Die from it. Surrender it. Reclaim it. Justify it. Blame it. Deny it. Just try it. Run from it. Embrace it. Model it. Fall for it. Become it.

And then hide from the only answer *to* it.

If we confess our sins, He is faithful and righteous to forgive us our sins and to cleanse us from all unrighteousness. -- I John 1:9

Confession is pretty much the opposite of hiding.

Now, to be "real," *not* hiding can be pretty lonely sometimes too. When I was habitually sinning and my depleted sense of self was searching for completeness through sexuality, I had many people in my life. I had those who knew the sinful me and accepted it as something beneficial to them. I had the closeness of those who knew nothing about my sin at all and accepted the face-value me. With me out of hiding now, many of both groups have run for cover. And . . . it gets lonely, as you will discover when you come from the darkness into the light and face the uncertainty of those who have discovered the "is it really true?" repentant you. The non-repentant ones who remain in darkness adopt a "who-are-you" attitude towards you because they no longer need you. Those who walk all the way through with you? What a gracious gift from God.

The light can be scary too. Things that were hazy in darkness can be brilliantly painful in the brightest light.

And then there is God. A redeemer. A restorer. A comforter. An ever-present help in times of trouble.

Don't hide. Cry to Jesus. He is there.

Sometimes the way is lonely,
And steep and filled with pain,
So if your sky is dark and pours the rain,
Cry to Jesus.
Cry to Jesus and live.

-- Chris Rice, Untitled Hymn

Every game eventually grows old and we come in to get warm or seek rest. Hide and Seek -- once all the good spots have been discovered -- is just no fun anymore.

Come to Me, all who are weary and heavy-laden, and I will give you
rest. -- Matthew 11:28.

All in, all in . . . all come free. All: you and me.
Hidden so well you can't find the way? Follow the light.

I have come as Light into the world, so that everyone who believes in
Me will not remain in darkness. -- John 12:46

CHAPTER 9

Thankful Even for the Pit

The blackness of eternal night encompassed me. I struggled for breath. The intensity of the darkness seemed to oppress and stifle me. The atmosphere was intolerably close. I still lay quietly, and made effort to exercise my reason. I brought to mind the inquisitorial proceedings, and attempted from that point to deduce my real condition. The sentence had passed; and it appeared to me that a very long interval of time had since elapsed. Yet not for a moment did I suppose myself actually dead. Such a supposition, notwithstanding what we read in fiction, is altogether inconsistent with real existence;—but where and in what state was I?

-- Edgar Allen Poe
The Pit and the Pendulum

When I was a little boy, Thanksgiving Day was the most definable day of the year. It was a day with no surprises: who, what, when and where were all determined by a cookie-cutter passed from generations before. The drive to the grandparents, the hugging aunts and uncles, the pesky cousins, the menu, the children's table, a toppled glass of tea, the games, the leaves in the yard, drawing names for Christmas, a chilly too-fast setting sun, falling asleep in the backseat on the way home. Same old, same old. Delicious comfort and continuity. There was an overwhelming rightness about all of it.

Much of it is still the same, sans the "when I was a little boy" part. The grandparents have passed on; the aunts and uncles are getting scarce, the cousins are less pesky, the sun still sets too fast and if I fall asleep on the drive home, it's all over. I was the little boy who toppled the tea . . . and I'm the man who broke the cookie-cutter.

It is the time we consider the things for which we are thankful.

Be joyful always; pray continually; give thanks in all circumstances, for this is God's will for you in Christ Jesus. -- I Thessalonians 5:16-18

To which, sometimes, I am inclined to say . . . *whatever* . . in the sense of casting this verse aside as inappropriately cheerful and inordinately inappropriate for me. Be joyful? Always? In *all* circumstances? Pray *continually* and give thanks . . . no matter what? And why? Oh . . . because it is God's will for me because I am in Christ Jesus . . . who died so I could.

But . . .

But what about this pit? Wouldn't it be acceptable to paint on a smile, brighten the old eyes, reconstitute the happy memories and . . . pretend? Does the joy have to be all real and everything? Can the thanks be canned . . . or does it have to be organic and fresh? Can I carve off a few of the circumstances like the lesser pieces of the turkey? Do I have to unclose my eyes?

"Give thanks in all circumstances."

Why are some parts of the Bible a bit of a mystery . . . but others so stunningly clear?

Which leads me to the next question: Is this pit really a pit at all?

One very nice April day, around mid-day, I tottered off the edge of it and plunged into the blackness of what seemed a never-ending free fall. It was the beginning of an "all circumstances" that stretches the veracity of God's Word . . . and yet . . . these many months later, I find myself oddly thankful.

On that very nice day, I was arrested in a city park while having lunch, while running an errand, while conversing with an undercover police officer, car-to-car, across the windows, words drifting slowly away from the innocence of the beautiful day to an unguarded expression of temptation. From tuna to handcuffs in a minute's time. From running an errand to rearranging life. From meetings with executives to sitting on a steel bench in a cinder-block holding cell with others who had been rounded up on a beautiful day because their sexual brokenness had broken them down and thrown them into a pit. If remorse and regret and disgust and despair were marketable, a fortune could be made in that dingy space of circumstance.

Within two weeks I was out of my job as an executive at AT&T. Shortly, I was removed from my church in an act of discipline, enacted in front of my already-estranged children who had been invited to watch, and in front of my Christian brothers and sisters who were told the church would prosper by removing me. The story of my arrest was page one news in the state's largest newspaper and on-line . . . accompanied by slanderous comments, untrue but unchallenged. People I had known for many years no longer knew me. There were places I could not, would not go. The bleak was upon me.

> *You were wearied by all your ways, but you would not say, 'It is* **hopeless***.' You found renewal of your strength, and so you did not faint. -- Isaiah 57:10*

My ways wearied me. His hope renews me.

I did find myself for awhile there much in the position of Eve, the devil taunting me with that small word "all" as he did Eve with the small word "any."

"Did God really say, 'You must not eat from *any* tree in the garden'?" "Did God really say, "Give thanks in *all* circumstances?" Ahhh ... the devil and his three-letter trip-ups. He loves doubt . . . as in *really?* Did God *really* say that? And, where God, through Christ, would give me hope and help, the devil would stir within me bent righteousness towards bitterness and anger, seeds of vengeance and justification, danger signs of refused repentance, roadblocks to block any path out of any pit, blinders to any speck of light.

Even though I could not be thankful for what had happened, I could be thankful that, despite my sin, Christ knows me and forgives me.

What has happened since my tripping into the pit? For one, I learned that churchianity is not always Christianity . . . but that we don't always know until we're outside what is missing on the inside, so I learned also not to judge too harshly, to be thankful for the peek and to seek a way to open other eyes, thus to encourage others to extend greater mercy to the fallen. I have learned that compassion provides the spark of energy for the fallen's foot to find the first rung on the ladder to freedom.

I have learned that while those who truly do love like the Lord are in the minority . . . . there truly are *some* who truly love like the Lord. And I have learned that many who don't, can't . . . because they need to be and aren't.

I have learned of sticks and stones and specks and logs . . . and I have learned we all have cluttered eyes and sometimes we clench our fists around stones to keep from hugging.

I have longed long enough for a life without longing. A perfect life with no pain and no pain-giving. A life where I have not tasted of every tree in the garden. But longing is not thanking.

My days are different now. No staff meetings. No PowerPoints. No schemes and defenses. No spin or talking points. No white papers. No business lunches . . . conferences . . . trips to plan. No annual raise, benefit package, stock option or bonus. No boss. There is less certainty in what the world has to offer and therefore more dependence on Him. My wife is my staff, my power lunch, my conferee. God is the only boss. He provides my bonus.

God has blessed me with the absence of these things, disastrous as the world measures, the cost of my brokenness in a world that fully embraces only wholeness . . . or at least the representation of such. Don't let it show . . . . let no one know.

I am thankful. I am even thankful for the sunny day plunge into the pit. Now I know. I know the darkness. Had I not, I would not know for certain the way out. And that, indeed, is something to be thankful for. And something to share with others who dwell there, thinking perhaps their plight is to reside among the rats until their bones form the floor onto which others fall. Now I know. I know that God's grace is even in that place. No matter how deep the pit . . . grace overflows from above and penetrates to the very depth.

> But the gift is not like the trespass. For if the many died by the trespass
> of the one man, how much more did God's grace and the gift that
> came by the **grace** of the one man, Jesus Christ, **overflow** to the many!
> -- Romans 5:15

I still pray -- every day -- that God will take away all these temptations and distractions and distortions that come from who knows where and who knows why. Just take away "who" and give me "know." I pray that my children will come back into my life, old friendships will be restored, bitterness and anger will subside. But I pray that as He does answer these prayers, He leaves the memories, even of the pain and sorrow and confusion, out of which arose my compassion for other strugglers and into which He poured His grace for me. I am so thankful.

Our sadder memories are perhaps the fertile plots from whence our mercy grows. Mercy we can pour out into the lives of those around us who may be skirting the edge . . . or exploring in tears the bottom . . . of a pit we cannot see but from which they cannot seem to escape. Mercy and grace are necessary rations for the climb.

> *"Be merciful, just as your Father is merciful. Do not judge, and you will not be judged. Do not condemn, and you will not be condemned. Forgive, and you will be forgiven. Give, and it will be given to you. A good measure, pressed down, shaken together and running over, will be poured into your lap. For with the measure you use, it will be measured to you. -- Luke 6:36-38*

Unclose your eyes . . . and be thankful. I am. The blackness of eternal night has been dispelled.

CHAPTER 10

RECLAIMING TATTERED INTEGRITY

Not what my hands have done can save my guilty soul;
Not what my toiling flesh has borne can make my spirit whole.
Not what I feel or do can give me peace with God;
Not all my prayers and sighs and tears can bear my awful load.

Your voice alone, O Lord, can speak to me of grace;
Your power alone, O Son of God, can all my sin erase.
No other work but Yours, no other blood will do;
No strength but that which is divine can bear me safely through.

-- Horatius Bonar, 1808-1889

I attended a 90th birthday celebration for my stepfather. Surrounded by his family and basking in their love, he was eventually reduced to tears of joy. Clear in his own remarks was the comfort of his awareness that he had generally lived life well and upright, as much as a man can in this fallen world. Not perfect, but comfortable in his knowledge of forgiveness and in his gratitude for grace. He felt the love and knew it was real.

The word "integrity" was spoken in reference to him and I found myself envying that, amazed that he had traversed nine decades and maintained his integrity in the minds of those who had seen him travel through.

On the drive back home, through a gentle rain and a descending darkness, I pondered my fewer decades and the truth of integrity-lost. In my life, I had not taken the road less-traveled. I had not even taken the more familiar path of the many. Wielding my self-made machete, I thrashed my way right through the middle of the overgrown thorny wilderness, and in the weariness of wandering through the tangled vines and thistles, I traded the good things for those that can weigh us down when we are determined to seek our own way. Including integrity. I made my own way, fashioning a route that reflected some unfortunate influences that came upon me, yet . . . I made my own choices.

Those of us who stray can certainly point to the occasional forced detour, but, ultimately we bear the responsibility for where we have been and where we are and where we will yet go. A light was always available on the darkened path; I often turned away from it as if it were a glare and not a guide.

Man seems so often to want the garden on his own terms. A little tending here and there to be rewarded by pleasures not planted for our benefit, but which entice us to lay aside the tools a bit and seek desperate respite. In creep the weeds, choking away what once nourished, until there is a barrenness that becomes a depleted and depressing landscape on poisoned soil. Integrity traded for skewed gratification or to fill a gnawing and misunderstood emptiness.

It is not for man to direct his steps. -- Jeremiah 10:23

That would be "any man." It was not right for me to direct my steps . . . or to choose steps in reflection of others' direction. I did both. I made choices to please myself on occasion and I made choices -- good and bad -- to please others. When I tried to emerge from the darkness, it was often because I was yearning for the good light of others, for approval. I would follow the direction of perhaps well-intentioned men – ministers -- rather than pursuing only God. The two can certainly align, but often do not. I would find myself so wanting to be seen as repentant and restored that I would agree to any plan set forth . . . just to have everything look right again . . . in the eyes of men.

"I promise," I would say. "I'll do whatever you say."

But I tell you, do not swear an oath at all: either by heaven, for it is God's throne; or by the earth, for it is his footstool; or by Jerusalem, for it is the city of the Great King. And do not swear by your head, for you cannot make even one hair white or black. All you need to say is simply 'Yes' or 'No'; anything beyond this comes from the evil one. – Matthew 5:34-37

I must be honest and say that I did not respect the men who established the plan, but I pledged to fulfill it anyway. I went from one long search for approval from men -- grappling with my broken sexual identity -- to another search -- thirsting for spiritual approval. From men. The evil one worked in both situations. The result? A doubling-down in my slipping search for integrity.

> *For am I now seeking the favor of men, or of God? Or am I striving to please men? If I were still trying to please men, I would not be a bond-servant of Christ. -- Galatians 9:10*

I wish I were more of a sponge when it comes to the Word of God. I would have done more than just heard that you cannot please God and man. I would have lived it.

I know many men and women are precariously picking their way through life among the sharp shards of a shredded and tattered integrity. This is not where we wanted to be. We find ourselves here because there were a lot of places we should never have been. The question is: can integrity be reclaimed?

Indeed, it can. The pieces can be re-fitted and re-arranged and sewn together to create a tapestry of integrity that reflects past struggles in the brilliance of blinding restoration. The broken can shine. God *does* bless the broken road. Pull to the side and wave the white flag.

We re-establish our integrity by re-tracing the steps of its loss.

1. Depend on God. -- A man or woman of integrity is someone who depends on God. I lost my integrity when I saw God as only a rescuer and not a rest. I did not rest in Him and wait on Him. I ran in front and called on Him when I fell in exhaustion. He was, of course, always there and I stood again because of His love, but I often left my integrity behind and ran on again.

2. Practice humility. -- This does not mean to perfect a *persona* of humility. It means "be humble." And, practice means just that: do it over and over until it becomes who you are. A man who seeks to satisfy himself without clarifying that satisfaction to be the will of God is not a humble man. I thought of myself as downtrodden at times because of a hunger; I sought to satisfy that hunger by whatever means pleased me. That is pride, not integrity.

3. Take responsibility for your actions. -- As I said earlier, many of us who have struggled with sexual issues were exposed to harmful circumstances or were not exposed to good teaching and direction. We need to deal with those realities through the process of forgiveness of whoever harmed us or neglected us . . . and then allow the grace of God to heal us. Thus healed, we are responsible for our own actions. The blaming of others only creates a greater circle of blame; it doesn't water down our own culpability. I've also discovered through time that most people don't really care that much what caused me to stumble. They just want me to walk upright. In integrity.

4. Be diligent in good things. -- Even the slightest amount of personal objectivity can lead us to a fairly accurate list of good and bad . . . if we are Christians. It's not hard to know when we are doing bad things. We feel convicted. We suffocate in guilt. We fall beneath the weight of shame. We retreat to blame. We shy away from God because we are embarrassed to be called a son of God. Each breath is labored; we deny ourselves access to the Breath of Heaven. A person of integrity breathes freely.

5. Be obedient to God. -- Often we confuse obedience to men -- even church leaders -- with obedience to God. If we are obedient to God, we won't have to worry about being obedient to church leaders. God will provide the grace we need to do so and the place we need to be in to make their yoke as light a burden as is His. I think when we refuse to be obedient to God, He allows us to be broken down through the heavy burdens of enforced obedience, inflicted by men confused by our brokenness. Please God. The rest will take care of itself.

6. Be honest . . . good-hearted . . . faithful . . . kind . . . gracious . . . gentle in spirit. -- Hiding in the swamp of sin is not honest. Being consumed with terror that others will see into the blackness of our heart is not being good-hearted. A double-life is not a reflection of being faithful; it is a sign of distrust in God. Being self-consumed makes us unkind. Pleasing ourselves above God and others is not gracious. Protecting ourselves and defending our impure ways detours a gentleness of spirit.

Does this seem like a difficult list? It's not. It is relief and rest. Can you imagine what it would be like to live a life dependent on an all-powerful God . . . to be humble and not worry about impressing others . . . to willingly accept responsibility for our actions and stand corrected and strong . . . to welcome accountability . . . to be diligent in doing good . . . to be obedient to God and guilt-free . . . to be honest and transparent . . . to love others and be called upon by them for help because of our open graciousness and gentle spirit?

Does it sound hard? Are you worn out by all the flailing about that is a part of our instinct for survival in this world? Do you feel alone in your struggle?

Come to me, all you who are weary and burdened, and I will give you rest. -- Matthew 11:28

We *can* walk in integrity. We are not bound by our past sins; we are not forced to move into a forced labor camp of legalism. We are invited to be partakers of grace. If someone is telling you that you can't reclaim your integrity, then pray for their faith, for it is lacking. They're telling you that God is not capable of restoring *you*. My fate rests in the hands of an almighty God, not an arbitrary one; a God who is more than capable of restoring me. A God who *loves me* and wants me back.

There is no "worst sinner." No matter what the weight is when we step out of the boat, the Hand extended bears us up.

At the end of the party, the 90-year-old man expressed his one wish. That everyone present live to be 90. I want to.

In integrity.

CHAPTER 11

WHY ARE YOU LOOKING
AT ME LIKE THAT?

There are times when I wish I could not close my eyes, beyond the need for sleep. Not only are they windows for my imagination, but they are too clear openings to real reminders of moments when I walked blindly. They hide nothing; reveal everything. To those who look at me, they are blue. From the inside though, from my view, they tend more to be grey, shadow-bound.

It's not the old "man-in-the-mirror" complex, although I have looked into my own eyes before and asked *"Why are you looking at me like that?"* Beyond the receding hairline, and a curiosity about whether my ears will ever even out with the rest of my face, it is the soul into which I see that has, more so in the past, troubled me. No creative facial expression fools me.

I used to go to a church where one of the members, a very nice man who was mentally challenged, did not, at some times, like to be looked at. You never knew for sure. Sometimes he was very approachable; sometimes he was intentionally distant. You were in his world only if invited. And, if not, he would say, with a threatening tone, "Stop looking at me!" He was not a little guy, so the warning was usually heeded. You were in only if you were invited in. I realized then, perhaps more than I wanted to admit, that his response was a defensive mechanism. He had obviously been hurt by those who had gazed at him as if he were not, somehow equal. He didn't want sympathy. He didn't want judgment. He just wanted to trust . . . and it was hard.

I understand that. No matter whether our pain and loss is self-inflicted, or whether it is just a quirk of nature or the result of someone else's

49

carelessness or uncaringness, those who struggle -- whether it is with sin or just a gnawing reality that they somehow don't measure up to those around them -- don't want to be looked upon as less. We can acknowledge our brokenness in the mirror; we can confess it to those we trust; we can turn it over to God . . . but we don't need the misery of visual judgment. Hence: *"Why are you looking at me like that?"*

I imagine my own sin has multiplied itself many times over, manifested in the growth of gossipers and the nourishment of the self-righteous. I have come to realize that there are a few people in my past that would not forgive me and believe me healed even if they were to be standing on a lakeside and see me walking on the water hand-in-hand with Jesus. I also have come to realize that there are plenty of people who just can't be bothered with a brother's redemption and repentance, not if it takes longer than they establish. This is a busy world you know; lots of things to plan, so much to see. We grow tired and seek new missions.

I test the waters on occasion and find that the anger is still strong. Having experienced the incredible and mysterious change that comes upon a Christian who passes through the mirror of self-hatred and into the loving acceptance of the One who knew us before, during and after . . . I want to ask again to those who don't know me now . . . but hold on to the me they knew when: *"Why are you looking at me like that?"*

But I realize they don't know me at all anymore, and I'm honestly okay with that. As they have memories of me; I have memories of them. I remember that some of them like what they see in the mirror a little too much. Honestly, some people, instead of being *like* God want to "*be* God." It's an odd blindness.

> *Who is a God like You, who pardons iniquity and passes over the rebellious act of the remnant of His possession? He does not retain His anger forever because He delights in unchanging love. He will again have compassion on us; He will tread our iniquities under foot. Yes, You will cast all their sins into the depths of the sea. -- Micah 7:18-19*

Jesus walked on the sea into which God is willing to cast our sins.

Why is it that some people would not walk across the street to help a broken man . . . yet God's Son would set aside his royalty and suffer and die? Why is it that some Christians today spend all their energy protecting themselves from being tarnished by the ones they judge unclean when Jesus went out of His way to assure them that He did not see them that way? He saw the broken in a wholeness He knew they could inhabit.

People who struggle with sexual brokenness are bombarded with opinions instead of truths. Some people say "accept your plight." Some say "accept your gift." Some say "God can change you; get back to me on that." Some say, "I love you and I will walk with you as Christ would." Others just say "I'll pray for you," and the struggler hopes they will, but many times already knows enough to have only a shred of confidence in that. In the mix of opinions, it is as if the struggler has many faces, depending on the fixated beliefs of the eyes that look upon him.

"Why are you looking at me like that . . . or that . . . or that?"

God bless those who cannot help but respond with eyes of love and mercy. In that is strength. Meet their gazes and draw from it. As to the others, you are under no obligation to stare them down; it's energy needed elsewhere.

Sympathy and empathy are empty without a belief in the power of Christ to heal and the Holy Spirit to lead believers out of the wilderness that, yes, does plague Christians. Christians who struggle with sexual brokenness are hiding out in the pews, alternately trembling from fear of discovery and need of wholeness. They want to be transparent, but they have experienced the wide-eyes of unbelief, either directly or through the conversations of Christians who mock the public strugglers, unaware that the man or woman next to them is drowning and would like a hand to reach out for . . . but is internally shrinking back, considering that it might be safer beneath the waves.

Again, Jesus walked on the sea into which God is willing to cast our sins. The church is populated with people who don't really believe that *Christ* can do all things, much less that those who believe in Him can, with His strength.

> *Therefore I say to you, all things for which you pray and ask, believe that you have received them, and they will be granted you. -- Mark 11:24*

Pray . . . ask . . . believe . .. receive.

Jesus is even patient when we struggle to believe. When we look directly into His eyes, we see reflected there our own pain and repeated failures and drop our heads from meeting His loving gaze. By His example of patience, we have to extend grace and patience ourselves to those who have closely recorded in their files and journals the records of our past stumbles. They believe in what they *see* and in their carefully-kept record of wrongs. Oddly, that evidence, even when weighed against the overwhelming evidence of generations of changed lives, is something to which they cling. Doubt becomes conviction, and overwhelms possibility.

> *And Jesus said to him, "'If You can?' All things are possible to him who believes." Immediately the boy's father cried out and said, "I do believe; help my unbelief." When Jesus saw that a crowd was rapidly gathering, He rebuked the unclean spirit, saying to it, "You deaf and mute spirit, I command you, come out of him and do not enter him again." -- Mark 9:23-25*

Help my unbelief. And . . . while You're at it, please help theirs.

So . . . how does one meet the mirror and walk away in peace? And how does one greet the naysayer and stroll on without bending beneath the weight of shame and guilt that comes when we know others know of our sin and brokenness?

By focusing on what God sees.

> *For You formed my inward parts; You wove me in my mother's womb. I will give thanks to You, for I am fearfully and wonderfully made; Wonderful are Your works, And my soul knows it very well. My frame was not hidden from You when I was made in secret and skillfully wrought in the depths of the earth; -- Psalm 139:13-15*

God's eyes beheld our soul before our mothers counted our fingers. God's eyes saw us stumble into our first mess. God's eyes watched us struggle deeper and deeper into the quicksand of our rebellion. God's eyes saw ours when they were flashing with defiance and brimming with remorse. God's eyes beheld our pride and saw our shame.

If we focus on what God sees, we may again ask, *"Why are you looking at me like that?"*

And the answer is, "Because I love you." Still.

When we find ourselves beached by the waves of our dismal memories, we need to realize that God's memories trump ours. He remembers when we were "wonderfully made" and "skillfully wrought." And He remembers the plans He had for us. If we turn to Him, forsaking all others, He blows the dust off the mislaid plans and puts the pieces back together and opens the gate again to point the way back to the path from which we turned.

Welcome God's gaze. He knows you. He knew whether your eyes would be blue, or green, or brown or a million other shades of His choice. He can remove the shadows that cloud our vision so we can see Him back. And He won't ask us why we are looking at Him. He knows.

CHAPTER 12

THIS WON'T HURT A BIT

There once was a shepherd boy who was bored as he sat on the hillside watching the village sheep. To amuse himself he took a great breath and sang out, "Wolf! Wolf! The wolf is chasing the sheep!"

-- Aesop's Fables

Some mornings the sunshine is so brilliant through my office window that I almost need sunglasses to focus on the keyboard. The cloudless sky spreads from a softness along the horizon to a taken-for-granted pureness at its unlimited heights above. The breeze is gentle and all seems as it is meant to be. The majesty of this morning reflects the truth of God, the control He has over all the earth and all within it.

But somewhere every morning there are clouds and rain and fierce winds. In other places, it is dry and hot and still. Still elsewhere, ice covers the earth for miles and much of life is forbidden. That too, expresses the truth of God and His control. Floods and droughts . . . . soft rains, cool breezes . . . searing heat. Where we are in a moment or space can make us wonder at that truth -- God's control -- and perhaps open ourselves up to the chance of becoming a victim of lies, a doubter of truth.

And the truth is, we are surrounded by peddlers of self-proclaimed wisdom, the most damaging of which often comes from pious observers who claim to have never been in a trench or pit, but are sure they know why others have and how we are either on our way to unavoidable suffocation . . . or supreme freedom. "If you just follow my guide," which often reads like the multi-language sheets that come with "some-assembly-required" purchases. All those tiny diagrams and lists of parts and tools and step-by-step instructions. And when you're finished, the question is simple: "What should I do about this cut on my thumb from the people-proof plastic packaging?" Or this tear in my heart from the plastic people?

White lies are pervasive in our society. We justify them because we know the truth hurts. With some discernment, a little white lie here and there *can* be a generous offering. But lies to prop up ignorance or justify judgment are more damaging than the most glaring and searing truth.

When I was a little boy, I remember lining up in the hallway to swallow down a sugar cube containing a dose of polio vaccine. The school nurse said I should, so I did. It was sweet. A couple of years later, I remember going in for a tetanus shot after stepping on a nail which penetrated my tennis shoe. The nurse said "This won't hurt a bit." I howled louder than I had when I stepped on the nail. Her little white lie felt like I was going to die. Two years ago after a significant surgery, I returned to the doctor's office to have the staples removed. The nurse looked right at me and said "This is going to hurt, so we might as well get after it and get it over with." It hurt . . . but I knew we were going to get after it and get it over with, and I appreciated the honesty.

Honestly . . . would it hurt that bad for us to just be honest with each other? Sexual brokenness—whether it manifests itself as homosexuality, sexual addiction, pornography, idolatry, adultery, self-satisfaction through masturbation or another form—hurts. It wreaks havoc. It can destroy the broken one and devastate the lives of those who are close enough to feel the impact of the personal implosion. In the meantime, while we debate whether it is too painful to be truthful, we let culture administer so much anesthetic that all affected become numb.

> *The villagers came running up the hill to help the boy drive the wolf away. But when they arrived at the top of the hill, they found no wolf. The boy laughed at the sight of their angry faces.*
>
> *"Don't cry 'wolf', shepherd boy," said the villagers, "when there's no wolf!" They went grumbling back down the hill.*

Sometimes the search of the broken begins with the cry for attention. The hurt of dressed-up dishonesty is magnified when the broken one lies to himself, in part because he buys into the lies of the ones who tell him that being broken is a *gift*. "You just need to learn to express your specialness." "Live the life you've been given." "Accept yourself as God made you." "Drop the denial; put down the mask; bask." What? Like a plane with no wings, destined never to leave the runway? Never to see the view from on high? If brokenness is a gift, would someone please provide the gift receipt so it can be taken back?

Later, the boy sang out again, "Wolf! Wolf! The wolf is chasing the sheep!" To his naughty delight, he watched the villagers run up the hill to help him drive the wolf away.

When the villagers saw no wolf they sternly said, "Save your frightened song for when there is really something wrong! Don't cry 'wolf' when there is NO wolf!"

But the boy just grinned and watched them go grumbling down the hill once more.

I can *almost* understand the failure of churches to offer real help and genuine truth to sexually-broken people. However, the word "failure" in that sentence overwhelms the word "almost." And the word "truth" trumps all. As it should. Sometimes crying wolf is just a practice round.

Too many times, churches -- and especially church leadership -- like to deliver the truth in a simple one-word package: "abomination." They say it as if they had never before seen a person in your condition, or as if it were an alternating verse in the Bible, interjected throughout to counter-balance all the ones about grace. If that's the case, then they must not understand the jokes they've been laughing at . . . or telling, about the abominably broken. I once had a minister appointed to be my accountability person tell me that he understood, cared and would walk with me all the way. I heard him also at a men's meeting, rousing the crowd with funny jokes about limp-wristed gay men. I knew full well that I was not the only man in the room who struggled with same-sex attraction. I was left wondering which pastoral persona was the truth: A counseling one-on-one or a group breakfast stand-up routine? Was he intentionally trying to be confusing? No. Was he clear on the truth? No.

Abomination above all abominations? Perhaps if you are ignorant, or fearful, or both.

And then you have the gay sympathizers. They don't want you to feel bad, so they dress your wounds with the balm of acceptance and affirmation. Not of you, necessarily. But of your brokenness. The balm is a curious concoction made from the watering down of the Gospel and the squeezing of the fruit of confusion. Rather than focusing on what the doctor (Jesus) ordered, they prepare a prescription based on what He did not. End result: you're not broken at all. Welcome to the island of misfit toys. Lie.

> *Later, he saw a REAL wolf prowling about his flock. Alarmed, he leaped to his feet and sang out as loudly as he could, "Wolf! Wolf!"*
>
> *But the villagers thought he was trying to fool them again, and so they didn't come.*

So, what *is* the truth?

The truth is that homosexuality *and* heterosexuality can result in very sinful behavior. Sexuality is a gift from God and heterosexuality is the package in which it is presented. Giving a pass to *anyone* who sins sexually is nothing more than cultural bias. Sexual sin is sexual sin. I personally think Jesus would have spent just as much time drawing in the sand for the homosexual as he did for the adulteress. And he would have given the same advice: "Go and sin no more."

There are those who want to attribute some Biblical approval for homosexuality that just isn't there. It's a feel-good philosophy that seeks to let misguided and hurting people off the hook, but doesn't set them on firm ground.

Don't fall for the fallacy that if Jesus had really cared about the issue of homosexuality, he would have been more specific. Jesus embraced scriptural truth.

Don't hide behind the eunuchs, who did not choose to be what they were forced to be.

Don't excuse yourself because you think the things you do are not that bad, as in "well, at least I don't . . . ." Sex outside of marriage is sin; the Bible is clear on that.

Don't wave the David and Jonathan banner. The Bible is clear that sexual relations between people of the same sex is sin. Why take an enviable and honorable and supportive friendship between two men and pervert it, just to make yourself feel better?

Don't.

Christians who just can't help themselves need to turn to someone who can. Jesus. It gets really hard to trust your life to Jesus if you change His Word to suit your needs.

Something else that is just *not* true is that this is a sexual addiction from which you can not escape. The truth is that you *can* be free of engaging in homosexuality, viewing pornography, having sex outside marriage, habitual masturbation-based fantasy and sexualized idolatry. But, it might hurt.

OK . . . it *will* hurt.

So, we may as well get after it and get it done.

Occasionally a music artist, a celebrity -- even a minister or leader in a church -- will make news by proclaiming themselves to be "out." The announcements are usually presented with appealing portraits, the peace of self-acceptance on their faces.

Freedom. The inner sorrow has been air-brushed away. Sometimes it is easier to surrender to whoever will listen than to continue to cry out.

At sunset, everyone wondered why the shepherd boy hadn't returned to the village with their sheep. They went up the hill to find the boy. They found him weeping.

"There really was a wolf here! The flock has scattered! I cried out, "Wolf!" Why didn't you come?"

When do we no longer cry out? When do we no longer turn toward those who do? I guess the answer to those questions would be similar to "When do we no longer pray?" And the answer is, when we have given up on God. Then we've bought the big lie, and all the little white ones no longer matter.

The truth is, if Christian men and women who struggle were not so afraid of the response they might receive if they were to turn to their brothers and sisters in the church, we might see a different kind of outing, the sprouting of wings on broken frames, the healing of festered wounds, the throwing open of secret doors, the safe embrace of Christian love. The peace of grace-acceptance. The bearable lightness of forgiveness. A chin-up countenance of clarity where once ruled a cast-down countenance of confusion.

If you are a struggler, don't give up. Don't proclaim yourself done. If you are a Christian who does not struggle, don't stick a fork in the struggler and make a declaration. If you want to turn him over to God, do it with determination, not with dismissal.

An old man tried to comfort the boy as they walked back to the village.

"We'll help you look for the lost sheep in the morning," he said, putting his arm around the youth, "Nobody believes a liar...even when he is telling the truth!"

Yes, I know the story interwoven is but a fable. Like a parable. But, the truth is, we have so mangled the truth that we have destroyed the trust. The broken patch themselves up and the rest of us either pretend to not notice the bandages, or we call 911 and have them carted off for someone else to deal with. How can we justify that?

Would you rather have a parable? Straight from the mouth of Christ?

But he wanted to justify himself, so he asked Jesus, "And who is my neighbor? In reply Jesus said: "A man was going down from Jerusalem to Jericho, when he fell into the hands of robbers. They stripped him of his clothes, beat him and went away, leaving him half dead. A priest happened to be going down the same road, and when he saw the man, he passed by on the other side. So too, a Levite, when he came to the place and saw him, passed by on the other side. But a Samaritan, as he traveled, came where the man was; and when he saw him, he took pity on him. He went to him and bandaged his wounds, pouring on oil and wine. Then he put the man on his own donkey, took him to an inn and took care of him. The next day he took out two silver coins and gave them to the innkeeper. 'Look after him,' he said, 'and when I return, I will reimburse you for any extra expense you may have.'

"Which of these three do you think was a neighbor to the man who fell into the hands of robbers?"

The expert in the law replied, "The one who had mercy on him."

Jesus told him, "Go and do likewise." -- Luke 10:29-37

One more truth: it's just not that hard. Love them like Jesus. Have mercy. Maybe you don't have all the answers, but being at a loss for words doesn't vanquish the broken from your list of neighbors. You can still lift the broken from the side of the road.

If you are the broken, don't be fatally discouraged by the numbers of the passers-by.

Take heart.

Someone will stop.

CHAPTER 13

The Unexpected Upside
of Rejection

Most of us can remember some event when we were younger . . . or perhaps
a time just yesterday . . . when we found ourselves outside looking in. The
last ones chosen for a team. No invitation to a party in our mailbox. A
phone call unreturned or a letter never acknowledged. A failed job search.
A turned-down loan. Or perhaps more seriously, direct rejection, perhaps
in the form of a response to our failings or our fallings. Laid-off. Removed
from fellowship. A relationship that unravels and fades away. There is the
message that we don't or can't measure up . . . . which leads us to believe
indeed we can't, so we stop trying.

Separation.
Loneliness.
Desperation.
Misguided searching for our place, somewhere to fit in.
Self-medication.

People who struggle with sexual brokenness -- pornography,
homosexuality, adultery, idolatry or another form -- often find themselves
doing deep and persistent inner searches in an attempt to understand why
they struggle at all. After all, it doesn't really make any sense. Struggling
on purpose would be akin to dropping yourself off the side of an ocean
liner just to see if you can dog-paddle to shore. It would be stupid. Big
sharks. Big waves. Big mistake. Yet, many people look at the struggler as
one who happily embraces his sin, wraps himself in it like a comfortable
blanket and refuses to relent . . . or repent. And . . . when it is sexual, a

Christian with the problem becomes the modern version of untouchable for the squeamish in the pews.

Rejection.

Rejection, for many a struggler, is the reason he struggles in the first place. That elusive search for acceptance can lead down many a dark path. But then, darkness becomes second nature to the one who yields to its twisted shadows and finds fleeting comfort there. Strangely, it is in this seeking of acceptance that the struggler eventually triggers his own self-rejection, adding himself to the list of those who have already placed him in the basement with the broken things of life. "Don't leave me" becomes "leave me alone."

I've never sought to simplify the reason I struggled. It was a complicated journey. Putting a finger on one single thing as the cause cheapens the depth of the disaster. Plus, it doesn't explain the reasons for others' struggles, those who took a different path entirely, yet ended up at the same point . . . a pointless, frustrating repetitive cycle. Still, I do know that rejection played a part for me. At least a part.

While I remember clearly my molestation as an eight-year-old in the trusted hands of a broken and twisted scout master -- I wasn't spared the memories by some self-induced amnesia -- I remember even more clearly the rejection I felt when he found another victim and tossed me aside, used and abused and confused. Rejected. And, as a eight-year-old, I watched from across the darkened room as he groomed his next victim. I was ashamed, but I also envied. This good rejection stung as bad as any other shunning.

And that's the downside of rejection. It sends us searching for someone who can fulfill us in some way and make us believe we are acceptable. In our search, we go crashing into our fellow walking wounded and combine our guilt and shame into a swirling cauldron that burns and stings and destroys. Refuge can't be found among the rejected anymore than acceptance can be found among the respected who have affixed our labels to us . . . as if we were immune to the mirror.

But then . . . there is the upside of rejection.

Rejection awakens you to the reality that the key they carry, which seems to symbolize acceptance, opens only certain predetermined doors. Conditional acceptance may lead you to a more comfortable closet, but the caretakers often carry brooms, not beacons. In the closet are the hoops through which you must jump to maintain acceptance, and you are ever-aware that the door that let you in is the one that will show you out.

This new closet may feel comfortable and comforting at first, but it becomes confining and choking as you realize it comes with its new scales of measuring. It is a waiting place. Prove yourself and remain. Fail? Depart for having swindled the kindness.

When your eyes adjust to the light, you realize it's where they store the broken things and hand-me-downs. Their acceptance of you is somehow different and distant. And dangerously familiar.

Unless, of course, the closet is lined with grace, which is potent in its protection of your rawness, much like the cedar in a closet keeps the moths from the precious garments. The sweet smell of grace clears your lungs and allows you to breathe in the new life-giving fragrance of forgiveness. The cool comfort of grace heals the burning scars and seeps away the power of past memories, the entrapment of the guilt and shame and leaves us able to see the renewal that comes from the right kind of rejection. The upside.

> *But now He has reconciled you by Christ's physical body through death to present you holy in His sight, without blemish and free from accusation. -- Colossians 1:22*

Now there is an "R" word the rejected need: "reconciled." Maybe for some of us, we must travel the weary road of rejection to find the resting place of reconciliation through the acceptance that Christ provides for the repentant.

After all, until we allow rejection of the old, we don't put on the new - - - new heart, new mind. Until we embrace rejection, we don't embrace renewal.

> *Therefore, if anyone is in Christ, he is a new creation; the old has gone, the new has come! -- II Corinthians 5:17*

Some of us take a long time to realize that our restoration does not come through men. In the stretch of that long time, we search for ways to convince others that the brokenness has somehow repaired itself and we are now acceptable. As we always have, we want to please. We accept the conditions and we work the plans and we hide the flaws in our recovery because we fear . . . rejection.

I got so good at looking like I was running the race that I forgot I was not even in the stadium. And it cost me dearly, to the point of reaching a point where there was nothing believable about me at all. I knew Christ, but I was so busy covering myself that I refused to realize He had covered it all for me.

In our well-meant attempts to fit in, we put our energy into looking the part, sounding the right way, reducing the suspicions and polishing the outside to an acceptable sheen that belies the truth that the brokenness lies just beneath the surface. No fix beyond the saving grace of God will suffice. No favor among men is powerful enough to sustain the difficult repair of the damaged soul.

> *He has showed you, O man, what is good. And what does the Lord require of you? To act justly and to love mercy and to walk humbly with your God. -- Micah 6:8*

And then comes the day when we stop our stumbling, exchange our suffocating closet for the realities of the cross and we find the acceptance that was shrouded all along by wandering and wanting the acceptance of those around us.

The upside of rejection that leads to renewal is the gift of restoration. I have become aware that because of the consequences of my sin, there are things I long to have back in my life that may never return. But I am also aware that God's love is endless and I am loved by Him and He will fill that emptiness with something new. God paid an incredible price for my salvation, and, no matter how rigorous the path to repentance may be, He knows the way around each rock and the way through each valley.

> *For I am the Lord, your God, who takes hold of your right hand and says to you, Do not fear; I will help you. -- Isaiah 41:13*

For those who struggle, there is the upside of rejection. When others turn away and when even you turn away from yourself, you find the peace that is indeed beyond all comprehension. Acceptance.

> *At one time we too were foolish, disobedient, deceived and enslaved by all kinds of passions and pleasures. We lived in malice and envy, being hated and hating one another. But when the kindness and love of God our Savior appeared, He saved us, not because of righteous things we had done, but because of His mercy. He saved us through the washing of rebirth and renewal by the Holy Spirit, whom He poured out on us generously through Jesus Christ our Savior, so that, having been justified by His grace, we might become heirs having the hope of eternal life. -- Titus 3:3-7*

What a loaded verse for the rejected: we can go from being foolish, deceived and enslaved, from being hated and hating ourselves. We can exchange rejection for mercy, be justified by grace and live in hope. Because of an awesomely generous God.

I'm sorry for the rejection you have experienced. But I am oh so thankful for the mercy and the grace and the hope, and it comes from Christ alone, lest any man boast.

This is not a search without end. That's the upside.

CHAPTER 14

The Distance Between Night and Day

And I can see a light that is coming for the heart that holds on
A glorious light beyond all compare.
And there will be an end to these troubles
But until that day comes
We'll live to know You here on the earth.

-- Matt Redman

In the soft moonlight of midnight, shadows dancing against the baby-blue wall of the nursery from a cottonwood tree moving gently in the nighttime breeze, it is party time. The baby is awake and searching for his toes, his pacifier, his blanket, his mommy or his daddy. He is ready for his day to begin; he wants to explore. Yes . . . in the soft moonlight of midnight. Smiling, cooing, laughing.

In the first 10 years of our marriage, Lisa and I had five babies: four boys and then, a daughter. It was common among them to go through a period when they would have their nights and days mixed up. The normal waking in the middle-of the-night with hunger pains or indigestion or a wet diaper was not a huge problem. You pick them up, hold them, mumble a few comforting words, or, if you're Lisa, sing a lullaby, play with their toes and hopefully they close their eyes before you do. That was all normal. It was the periods when they ignored the realities of time and began their day in the middle of my night that were hard.

With all their potent body language—whether red-faced bawling or cherub-faced giggling—they would say with all the force of an eight-pounder: "You are not putting me down." "You are not leaving me in this dark room."

And we didn't. Not on those occasions where we knew the baby was just a bit mixed up; confused about the distance between day and night, oblivious to dark and light. These were not "I want" moments. These were "I need" times.

Sometimes we just need to yield ourselves to the "care for me" and "care about me" cries of those around us who are confused, even if our more common-sense mode tells us that perhaps we should just give them a pat on the back, flip the light back off and close the door. Cry your way through it; you'll be better for it. *I'm tired.*

Oh no, You never let go
Through the calm and through the storm.
Oh no, You never let go
In every high and every low.
Oh no, You never let go
Lord, You never let go of me.

-- Matt Redman

Sometimes we are the crying child and sometimes we are the comforting one who flips on the light and stays at the side of the weeping and the wailing and the gnashing. And sometimes we're the child who lies awake and refuses to call out, or the busy and self-absorbed who walks straight down the hall and past the room in which the bewildered toss in fits and turns.

And then, there's God. He *never* lets go. His perfect love casts out fear. Sometimes we don't see it because of the shadows that cast strange thoughts within our minds, but He is *always* there.

The Lord himself goes before you and will be with you; He will never leave you nor forsake you. Do not be afraid; do not be discouraged. -- Deuteronomy 31:8

Can you **imagine** what it would be like to go into our battles and **know** -- despite the pounding of our hearts and the furious flow of adrenalin -- that someone is at each shoulder, on our left and on our right, at every step? What if we knew that there was someone right in front of us, fully armed and determined to take the charge? What if we had the assurance that behind us is someone who will catch us if we fall, and move before us so the battle we think is lost becomes a victory instead?

Imagine . . . and know.

I remember watching the movie *Gettysburg* a few years back. I'm not a huge Civil War buff and I have no desire to march in a re-enactment, but there is a stunning moment from that movie that has favorably haunted me from the time I saw it. It has even been re-enacted in my dreams, which is as close as I want to get to the reality of it.

I don't remember the name of the particular battle which gripped my attention, but I can't forget the scene. It is a pivotal moment and will turn the war. Two armies -- the North and the South -- awake from a night of encampment and begin to prepare for the major battle that will cost many of the brave men their lives. The armies will meet in the clearing, each marching out from the cool covering of the woods, the dark, shady comfort of the trees, into the blazing sun, bayonets at the ready, muzzle-loaders hoisted.

My mind always says. "Don't go!" Stay in the shade. Turn around. Hunker down. Maybe the enemy will go away.

They don't listen to me.

The men line up in formation, shoulder-to-shoulder, and await the command to move. It comes. They look into each other's eyes one last time and then focus on the eyes of the enemy, coming out of cover and heading for the clearing. And they move straight toward the enemy, aware that at some point they will be in hand-to-hand combat and one army will declare the clearing held.

Shots ring out. Men fall on the left and on the right and the fortunate ones march on, stepping over and around the bodies of the fallen. Soon, the closeness of the armies makes the long rifles useless to fire and the enemy begins to stab and thrust with bayonets. Before the battle is over, men are downing each other one-on-one with knives pulled from their belts. And many fall and die, wondering as they hit the dusty field whether they have done enough to protect their loved ones.

In the end, one army stands, depleted and exhausted, but victorious, despite the huge losses inflicted on them. Great sorrow is experienced in a determination for victory.

I don't like battle. I like the clear-blue skies unencumbered by the dark and emerging clouds that creep from the horizon and blunt the sun. I don't want to be close enough to look into the eyes of the enemy; maybe that's why he so often creeps up behind me.

What if our lonely marches toward the seemingly never-ending walls of defiance that threaten to annihilate us in the middle of the clearing are not really lonely marches at all?

Imagine . . . and know.

The Lord Himself goes before you and will be with you; He will never leave you nor forsake you. Do not be afraid; do not be discouraged. -- Deuteronomy 31:8.

The Lord Himself? Before us and with us? He never leaves? And yet, He knows we become afraid and are sometimes discouraged. That sometimes our days and our nights are so mixed up that we are in a constant swamp of grayness. That sometimes we want to cast aside our armor and just dig a hole and hide. He *never* leaves.

Sometimes God comes to us and meets our outstretched hands in moments of exploration as we seek to discover our place in the world. And He speaks in a quiet still voice. At other times, He stands before us and all around us in full battle gear as we gasp for our survival. And He goes through the rage with us as the enemy strikes and we risk stumbling to our faces flat in the field. He *never* leaves.

God is never confused about night and day. Evil and good. Truth and deceit. No clever costuming by the enemy can fool God. He knows the serpent's voice and is immune to its cleverness.

We could learn a lot from God.

Like the sacrificial soldiers, we must stand with each other so we can take the clearing instead of retreating to the woods. I'm sure some of those soldiers were more combat-ready and better-trained than the others, but they all marched in. Some were probably already wounded from earlier battles. Some may not have slept the night before, robbed of rest by apprehension. Some may not have even liked the man on his left or right. Some may have been saints; others bound by sin. Yet, there they were, there for each other. Judgment could wait. Condemnation was on hold. They were too busy pointing bayonets in unison at the enemy to point fingers at each other. They were more determined to be a mighty army themselves than to shoot the wounded among them.

The church could learn a lot from them. And from God.

The army marches forward to victory because the weaknesses of each are overwhelmed by the combined strength of all. Even though the battlefield will sometimes melt down into chaos and confusion, the clarity of the mission remains.

Whether we are in the nursery wanting nurturing or in the clearing wanting a co-clobberer to enable our courage, we need to move forward.

We need a clarity of mission. We need to know where we want to be so we can make provision to get there, whether we limp across or leap across or get carried across.

We need to realize we don't live in a barn. I remember when I was a kid, my mother would sometimes peek into my room and tell me to get it cleaned up. "You don't live in a barn," she would say. I've thought about that in other ways. We talk so much about God opening doors, or we pull out the old saying that "when one door closes, He always opens a window." And these things are true. But, shouldn't we be *closing* a few doors in the meantime? Saying no to old habits and bad thinking? Eliminating destructive relationships that the enemy uses in our lives?

We need to be stronger for others. Those of us who struggle need to make darn sure that we are not enabling other strugglers. It is neither kind nor compassionate to play games along the edge of a cliff, to expose ourselves to temptations, to trim the hedges low enough to jump over, to put open spots in the boundaries, to keep relationships intact when we know we are headed for a fall. And I see that, all the time. People rarely fall alone. If you are a co-enabler, you're in co-denial.

We need to be ready to cross the bridge. One of my mother's -- and perhaps every harried mother's -- favorite sayings was "We'll cross that bridge when we get to it." I often told my own kids "We'll *jump off* that bridge when we get to it." "When we get to it," is the dangerous part of the phrase. The men at Gettysburg knew the clearing was ahead. They paused, planned, tried to rest, shared a meal, strengthened themselves as best they could, cleaned their armor, organized and pledged to cross the clearing . . . all before they came to it. And they knew well in advance when they would "get to it."

When I was a little boy, the directions for crossing a street were to look both ways twice and then cross. It was less scary if a crossing guard was there, but it was nice to know that if the guard was not present, I knew what to do. As I got a little older, I found myself crossing in the middle of the block so I wouldn't have to wait on that crossing guard. And, on occasion, even if I did look both ways, and even if it wasn't exactly clear, I would dart out into the street and dodge a car or two and leap to the opposite curb. I had decided that the instructions were too much trouble and the crossing guard way too slow. It is "my" life, after all. I can do with it what I want.

Then Jesus said to His disciples, "If anyone wishes to come after Me, he must deny himself, and take up his cross and follow Me. For whoever wishes to save his life will lose it; but whoever loses his life for My sake will find it. For what will it profit a man if he gains the whole world and forfeits his soul? Or what will a man give in exchange for his soul?" -- Matthew 16:24-26

My life? Mine? Not so much.
We can learn a lot from Jesus.

My brothers, if one of you should wander from the truth and someone should bring him back, remember this: Whoever turns a sinner from the error of his way will save him from death and cover over a multitude of sins. -- James 5:19-20

This was written to Christians with the full awareness that they were surrounded by people who might wander away from the truth and into the darkened room of deceit, an often-fatal error. We should be saying: "Not on my watch."

No matter how dark the room, He will not leave us in it. We may refuse to walk into the clearing with Him, but it will be our decision, not His. He is the light that shines in the darkness. He bridges the distance between night and day.

CHAPTER 15

WHAT SHOULD WE DO WHILE WE'RE WAITING?

Chaos: unpredictability; a state of confusion
Calm: period or condition of freedom from storms; a state of tranquility

I think I have not been good at waiting. But wait . . . let me think about that a bit. No, I can't wait . . . I don't really have time to think about it. Besides, I *know*. I'm *not* good at waiting. I like to plan and push and expect and get. If there's an answer out there, I don't want it held back from me. I do not like to anticipate or wonder. I'm a good wanderer, but a very poor waiter. I plunge headlong into chaos rather than cautiously wading into the calm. As much as I yearn to rise up with wings like an eagle, I have a greater tendency to scurry on in like a common sparrow. Thank God, literally, that His eye is upon me.

Are you waiting on some answers right now? Yearning for some peace within some plaguing issues? I cautiously wade into waiting, but I tend to pick up speed . . . my own speed . . . my own way . . . my own timing . . . and . . . if I do so, achieve my own results. My, oh my, that's a lot of "my."

One problem with waiting is that it so often seems that things truly are not worth the wait. I once sat up all night on Christmas Eve listening to a hamster wheel turning beneath the Christmas tree. I wanted that little hamster so, so badly. Cute and funny to watch, but definitely not worth the wait. Hamsters are clearly over-rated. I became a slave to a quarter-pound fur ball. Clean my cage; fill my bottle; get me treats; find me under the refrigerator as flat as a fridge magnet; bury me in the backyard.

Some things *are* worth the wait; that is for sure. Broke as could be, barely able to pay the bills and put shoes on our five kids, Lisa and I used to drive to a rise on the edge of the city and park in the middle of a pasture and wait on the time that we would be able to buy the land on which we built a house in which we now live. We waited. It took years . . . and now we've lived here for years and been blessed. We waited.

But what about those things in our lives that are not so tangible? What about when we are waiting for sorrow to be vanquished? Or for addictions to release their grip? Or for loneliness to leave? Or for pain to subside? Or for forgiveness to be real? Or for unwanted desires to diminish? Or for painful memories to fade? Or for change? Or for comfort? Or for strength? These are not squeaky presents under a tree. These are not things that can be processed through a bank loan. These are things we pray for. And sometimes, we wait longer than we want.

In our haste to impress upon God that there is no need to wait, we may go through stages ranging from paralysis to rage, from almost refusing to live at all . . . to living large and free, daring Him to stop us from our self-destruction. Sometimes we declare our own answers, do our own searches, make our own plans and move on our own understanding and with our own self-approval . . . just . . . tired of waiting. And when we suffer the consequences, we wait again, this time determined to let God work, even as we feel that fidgety need to fix it again.

Prone to wander, Lord I feel it.
Prone to leave the God I love.
Here's my heart, oh, take and seal it.
Seal it for Thy courts above.

-- Come, Thou Fount of Every Blessing

I am clearly "prone" to do quite a few things; waiting being the exception. But, if we would but wait . . . then what should we do while we're waiting, to keep us from acting on what we are *"willing?"* Oh, that silly will. It works like a weed-eater on our waiting.

Those of us who struggle with various types of personal brokenness know it is a matter miles beyond the will. I hear daily of men and women who plunge headfirst into the free-fall of free will and their determination to find wholeness diminishes into despair and a tearful longing for forgiveness and restoration. The good news is, as we wait upon the Lord for the answer, we are replenished through grace and we receive that forgiveness and restoration. That's what our will *should* seek.

What to do? What to do? First of all . . . we have to make sure we really are waiting on God . . . and not on someone else . . . or even on ourselves. I have to admit that for years I grappled with my sexual issues with the gnawing thought that there was no answer; that I had been given a perpetual ticket on a roller-coaster and all the attendants had gone home for the season. The park was closed. The die was cast. Get used to the butterflies in the stomach and the nauseating reality that you are going no-where.

Waiting is faith. Waiting believes that God has an answer and that God has no off-season.

I'm waiting for several worth-the-wait things right now. God knows. For one, I'm waiting for God to restore my family. And I'm rightly waiting, having run the gamut of the wrongful waits. I thought perhaps I could restore it myself. Nice long detour that was. I thought perhaps my church could do it. I thought I could out-wait my children. Out-waiting is one of the most wasteful waits of all. Mighty is the moment when we finally realize that some things can only be accomplished through waiting on God. In that knowledge, we can wield the power of waiting, and in wielding, discover the power of faith. Certainly, He *can* use me, my children, my church . . . or anything or anyone He wants to end the wait with an answer. I'll wait and see. Clearly I can not out-wait the Creator of time.

> *The Lord is the everlasting God, the Creator of the ends of the earth. He will not grow tired or weary, and His understanding no one can fathom. -- Isaiah 40:28*

God does not give up on us, though we often give up on Him, wearing ourselves out because we demonstrate waiting by entering a catatonic state of nothingness. Done properly, waiting strengthens us and we grow. Done poorly, we resemble mushrooms in a dark forest. We think waiting means doing nothing. But, back to the original question: What should you do while you're waiting?

> ***Have Hope*** *-- What strength do I have, that I should still **hope**? What prospects, that I should be patient? -- Job 6:11*

Job raised a good question during his long and painful period of waiting. God restored not only his hope, but everything he had lost.

Practice Patience -- *We want each of you to show this same diligence to the very end, in order to make your hope sure. We do not want you to become lazy, but to imitate those who through faith and **patience** inherit what has been promised. -- Hebrews 6:11-12*

God's promises are real; He has plans for us. Good ones. We need to be patient and await the inheritance.

Trust -- *When I am afraid, I will **trust** in you. -- Psalm 56:3*

Waiting is a scary journey, no matter what you're hoping for. For those who are awaiting a light in a walk to freedom along the pockmarked path of failed beginnings and elusive endings trust is a must.

Obey -- *This is love for God: to **obey** his commands. And his commands are not burdensome, for everyone born of God overcomes the world. This is the victory that has overcome the world, even our faith. -- John 5:3-4*

Aren't most of us longing to be loved? And can any love be greater than that exchanged between man and God? And well . . . overcoming is what we long for.

Which brings us back to waiting.

My path to today is littered with the longings of yesterday. So many of the things I once waited on are so far into the past now that I have forgotten even why I wanted them or what they were; some of them are no longer even valuable to me, their fate forever resigned to the "not-worth-the-wait" category.

Now I am waiting. Waiting for His voice, for His plan, for His direction. And I am hoping, and trusting and obeying. It will be worth it. He knows my needs; He knows my deeds. He loves me still. My God is faithful. And so is yours.

Just you wait and see.

CHAPTER 16

THE PROPER CARE AND FEEDING OF A WHY

It's okay to question why.
It's okay to even cry.
Don't ever hesitate to try.
God will answer; He won't lie.

There's no answer He won't know.
There's no place He will not go.
There's no path He will not show.
God will answer; He loves you so.

No question lies within your mind.
That God cannot in love unwind.
That's how we've all been so designed.
To seek from Him what we can't find.

In His answers lies our peace.
In His words, we find release.
Our search can end, our troubles cease.
It all begins with show me . . . please.

It's okay to question why.
It's okay to even cry.
Don't ever hesitate to try,
God will answer every sigh.

-- Thom Hunter

I remembered a "why" the other day that I wanted once to ask my Dad when I was just a little boy. It had to do with frogs, and it remains unanswered. Curious, like all children, I was filled with "why" questions. In this particular instance, it had to do with frogs because we had been out gigging frogs on a Texas pond in the dark mosquito-clouded night. The frogs were croaking like crazy and easy to trace down and stab to provide for tomorrow's fried frog leg breakfast.

I wanted to know why they were croaking so loud when they knew we were coming after them in the boat. And I wanted to know why there was no-where for them to go but this pond . . . or the frying pan. Why didn't they climb up the banks and go over the hill and hop along to a different pond, a safer place?

I think instead that I asked Daddy why there were more stars in the country sky than in the city . . . and I'm pretty sure he answered that one. But the frogs remained a mystery, drifting into the memory of a million "whys" I never got to ask. I probably yawned and scratched a bite or two and we went to shore and left the why of the frog behind on a crowded lily pad.

If I had a million whys for my dad . . . can you imagine the gazillions that drift heavenward? How many times must God have heard "Why, God?"

Why me?

Why this?

Why not?

Why won't they?

Why confess?

Why change?

Why repent?

Why is it still here?

Why again?

Why haven't you?

Why haven't *they*?

Why haven't *I*?

Why try?

Why resist?

Why flee?

Why . . . why?

Why, God?

I had five children. They always wanted to know why. Why can't we go there? Why do we have to go here? Why can't I have this? Why do I have to have *that*? Why doesn't it work? Why can't we afford it? Why do the leaves fall?

Why did you? Fall.

Sometimes when they were little, after an exhausting round of explaining why this and why that, the eventual bottom-line would be reached: "Because I said so."

God does the same thing sometimes. He says "Be still . . . and know that I am God." I think that's a lot like "Because I said so."

Sometimes we take really good care of our whys. We build fences and haul in feed and water and brush the coats and protect them like our favorite pets. This one is not getting loose. I kinda' like "why me?" My favorite.

And God says, "Be still."

But what about *this* why and *that* why?

"Be still."

Obviously God has always known of our propensity to find the nearest slippery slope and try it out like some new ride at Six Flags, ready to give it a rating at the end of the track. Man . . . that was fast, that was bumpy, that was quite a ride . . . awesome experience . . . freaky . . . deadly.

"Be still."

But God . . . when I am still, my mind is filled to overflowing with whys. I need to keep moving. At least when I'm on the slope I don't have to figure out all those answers to all those whys.

"And know that I am God."

When my children would not give up on asking all their whys to wear me down, I usually responded with a distracting promise: "Want a cookie?" I think today's parents probably pop in a video. Same thing. Distract. Deflect. Divide and conquer.

God says, *"Know that I am God."* He doesn't deflect or distract; He draws us right in to Him and reminds us He knows the answer to every why. And every "why me?" He knows me better than I know myself so when it comes to trusting and obeying, it really makes no sense to ask "why?" But, I do.

There's really only one answer. *For God's glory.* Why me? *For God's glory.* Why now? *For God's glory.* Why not? *For God's glory.* Why confess? *For God's glory.* Why repent? *For God's Glory.*

But there's a few nagging whys that surely tempt God to want to just lean across the seat and say "Want a cookie?"

Not God.

What about the "why again?" Answer: because you haven't transformed your mind.

Do not conform any longer to the pattern of this world, but be transformed by the renewing of your mind. Then you will be able to test and approve what God's will is -- His good, pleasing and perfect will. -- Romans 12:2

What about the "why won't they forgive?" Answer: Forgive *them*.

Then Peter came and said to Him, "Lord, how often shall my brother sin against me and I forgive him? Up to seven times?" Jesus said to him, "I do not say to you, up to seven times, but up to seventy times seven." -- Matthew 18:21-22

What about "why is 'it' still here?" or "why haven't You?" Answer: My grace is sufficient.

Three times I pleaded with the Lord to take it away from me. But He said to me, "My grace is sufficient for you, for My power is made perfect in weakness." Therefore I will boast all the more gladly about my weaknesses, so that Christ's power may rest on me. -- 2 Corinthians 12:8-9

I guess we could even ask "why so many whys?" Why does God put up with all this?

I remember when I was in various art classes in my early years. I tried leather and bought a wallet kit. Every time I would strike the tool with the mallet that was supposed to impress a neat capital "T" and "H" on my western wallet, the mallet would bounce and the lettering would look like stuttering. Very unintentionally artistic. I just wanted to toss the wallet in the scrap heap. I tried to make a bowl once out of clay. I saw two choices with my bowl: toss it back into the mud while it was still wet or toss it onto the floor after it dried. There's clearly a reason I was not called to be the creator of the universe.

And here we look at a world wrapped in ungrateful "whys" with the scary knowledge that He created everything that is by just speaking it into existence. "Be" and it was. "Be not" and it could be like a mis-shaped brittle bowl tossed onto a concrete floor, pieces flying to the four walls.

Why not?

Because He loves me. And He loves you. And he would rather answer the "whys" by slowly unwrapping the chains and setting us free a heartbeat at a time through His unending love and amazing grace until we see ourselves unencumbered and standing free . . . and asking "why?"

Because He loves. In all the good things He gives me and for all the bad things through which He sees me, He loves me. And as much as I sometimes hate this world that seems determined to hunt me down and pierce my soul with "whys," I have to remember . . .

For God so loved the world that He gave His one and only Son, that whoever believes in Him shall not perish but have eternal life. -- John 3:16.

I ask why and instead of a cookie, He gives me His son. Why would I ever think it was not enough?

Why?

CHAPTER 17

HAS ANYONE SEEN MY BURDEN?

What kind of clown am I?
What do I know of life?
Why can't I cast away
This mask of play
And live my life?

-- Stop the World - I Want to Get Off (1961 Broadway Musical)

I don't think we realize when we have picked up the burdens we may carry throughout our lives. If we saw them on the side of a road somewhere, we might slow down and ponder, stroke-our-chin, glance into our eyes in the rear-view mirror, even stop and shift into park, and then, all things duly-considered, drive on to leave them for some clean-up crew to handle. If we saw them on a shelf for sale, we might jingle the coins in our pocket or almost pull out the debit card, consider that we would have to dust them and arrange them if we took them home, realize they just eventually become so-much clutter, so we might admire them on the shelf and walk away. If someone offered them to us on a street corner, we might graciously nod and decline with a "no thanks, I don't really need that," and cross to the other side.

But we don't find them sitting in the sun on the side of the road on a Sunday drive through the countryside . . . or on the sale rack in the store beneath a sign that reads "Burdens at Rock-Bottom prices," or in the outstretched hands of a stranger at the curb saying "please take this."

We accumulate our burdens in much more subtle ways, a stumble here and there, a curious foray into unexplored territory, a letting down of the guard in a needy moment. Or maybe, as we journey along, some of them are crammed into our backpacks by someone else when we were momentarily distracted, or given to us in change returned during a misguided selling of our soul. Regardless, we pack them in and carry them on, a collection that weighs us down and saps our strength, sometimes bringing us to our knees. We shift them on occasion for comfort . . . and perhaps we ourselves sit on the curb and offer them to others, but we keep them nonetheless. Sometimes they're shared and diminished a bit; sometimes they're shared and multiplied.

I picked one up through another's "generosity" in the early '60s when I was sexually abused. He had enough burdens to divide them among others and he gave me my share and soon went on down the road to gift his burdens to others to bear, laying us down like little mile-markers along the road on his descent into darkness.

I picked another one up in the early '70s. It disguised itself as an answer to a gnawing need instead of as the key to an open door to a hell-on-earth. Once I walked through that door and stepped inside, despite my natural inclination to flee, I discovered an equally-natural inclination to hang on to that burden to serve as a doorstop to keep the door behind me open so I could return whenever that gnawing might lead me back down the path.

Our burdens intertwine and strengthen each other and almost always present themselves as answers, not roadblocks. Before we realize they're burdens, they seem more like gemstones. Like a hapless contestant on a game show who makes the choice to open one more briefcase or go to the next round of challenge, we often lose all because we are grasping at what seems so rewarding. We want more. For many of us, the need to be needed, the want to be wanted, the longing to be longed for, the desire to be desired, the craving for acceptance, the purely innocent comfort of not being rejected, the being noticed, the addiction of affirmation, the fuel of "love" -- phony or not—propels us into over-achievement in our burden-collecting.

For me, the door opened on a foggy corner in the drizzle of a past-midnight walk on a college campus when the door of a Volkswagen opened and a smiling driver offered me comfort and a dry ride out of the soaking night of self-pity and loneliness in which I was wandering, self-absorbed, but presenting myself like a sponge, daring someone to care about me. And he did. And I allowed it. And I left a little block of burden in the doorway so I could return when again the gray descended and the fog rolled in. I thought, "no harm."

Or perhaps I didn't really think at all. That's the thing about burdens. The care and feeding of them becomes so consuming that we find little time to consider the process of unencumbering ourselves until we are so cumbered we cannot spare the energy. We must instead figure out how to make sure no one sees what we are carrying. We rationalize at some point that no one *wants* to see them. There is no curb on which to sit; no garage sale to hold; no bargain-basement low enough. They're ours.

Much like watching a tree grow outside my office window—from wind-bending sapling to steady, shady oak—we don't see how our burdens grow. We've stashed them into a sack of secrets that, though invisible to others, becomes so heavy it nevertheless presents us to them as someone stooped in soul. They may not know why; they may suspect; they may have ceased to care, having been whacked here and there by a cloaked burden that fell from the pack through our clumsy packing and shifting.

Then again, a well-meaning hand may reach in on occasion. Looking into our eyes after just a glimpse into our box of burdens, he asks "What do you have in there? Can I help you with that?"

Like a threatened child with a favorite toy, we may have responded with a confusing mix: "These are mine! I mean, there's nothing there." And we resolve that no one will catch us lazily laying the stack within their reach again. And we close a door, a door through which someone may have been trying to squeeze because of their own prodding of the Holy Spirit to go beyond the threshold and walk into our lives.

Carry each other's burdens, and in this way you will fulfill the law of Christ. -- Galatians 6:2

But wait a minute, we say. My burden is not like the others. It's not a house blown-down by a hurricane. It's not a lay-off. It's not the sorrow of a family-member's untimely death. It's not a cancer cutting short my life. It's not a broken marriage. It's not a sick child or a parent with Alzheimer's. It's just not one of those recognizable burdens. It's. It's. It's . . . a giving in under the weight of a sin I can't seem to . . . bear. Like a burden? And we look at our ugly burdens, which somehow not only lost their shine, but turned black and moldy. And we think about the grime and the mess that might rub off if someone gets too close and tries to bear with us. "No." And we renew our determination to keep the lid on and prevent future spills.

Then, one day, like a defective oil rig, an explosion occurs and some get hit full-force by the crud. Others stand helplessly by and try to dodge the seeping and the spewing. Others project the long-term damage yet-to-come. Others point their fingers and levy their penalties.

But the burden is still there. Uglier than before, wider and deeper, spreading out no matter how hard we try to gather it back up; the sack in which we carried it is torn and useless, and one by one the burdens tumble out into full view. We trade shrinking beneath their weight, to crumbling at our fate, a new burden spawned by the vanquishing of secrecy.

This is a pivotal moment where some give up and some give in. Instead of giving away.

In the mid '70s, about the time I was learning to hide and bear, I was gripped by a song by Chuck Girard called *Lay Your Burden Down*. It played over and over in my head, but I also bore another burden, a refusal to trust. "I just can't do that," I would tell myself, each time I would loosen the tie upon the bag. "I can't lay this burden down. Not this one." And I would retreat, usually through a door of escape I had left open to keep me from entering the healing realm of transparency. Blast my resolve.

> *You've been tryin' hard to make it all alone*
> *Tryin' hard to make it on your own*
> *And the strength you once were feelin'*
> *Isn't there no more.*
> *And you think the wrong you've done*
> *Is just too much to be forgiven*
> *But you know that isn't true*
> *Just lay your burden down, He has forgiven you.*
>
> *-- Chuck Girard, 1975*

We think the wrong we've done is just too much to be forgiven? Maybe that is why we don't lay our burdens down, but instead wait until they are laid out, spilled like an overturned truck on the interstate, news helicopters hovering overhead, while we head for the ditch to hide.

Another burden we bear is the thought that we have gone beyond the limits of forgiveness. When we take inventory of the precious burdens we have protected, we are blinded by the enormity of them. We fall into the trap of thinking that Christians—limited by their constant brushes with the reality of earth—represent the limits of heaven. There are none.

If we don't accept the truth of forgiveness, we'll just keep replacing our burdens with the familiar lies that prompted our collecting in the first place. We'll be looking for looks of love in all the wrong faces.

Open the sack: *If we confess our sins, He is faithful and just and will forgive us our sins and purify us from all unrighteousness. -- 1 John 1:9*

Lay them out: *Have mercy on me, O God, according to Your unfailing love; according to Your great compassion blot out my transgressions. -- Psalm 51:11*

Leave them there: *As far as the east is from the west, so far has He removed our transgressions from us. -- Psalm 103:12*

Replace the memories of the bearing: *Their sins and lawless acts I will remember no more. -- Hebrews 10:17*

I think many times, for those of us who struggle with something so deep and penetrating as a war within ourselves, that we think that other people, or even God, are the daunting wall that blocks our paths to freedom. Often, it is instead a wall of mirrors, reflecting back to us the choices, the walks down blind alleys, the decisions in the dark. We don't, or won't, forgive ourselves. We know there are consequences for sins and we think that chief among the consequences are these burdens we just have to bear.

No.

God says we can lay them down. In the meantime, the Word says our brothers and sisters in Christ can help us bear them. If it takes a little traveling, even a stumble here and there, to get the burdens to the Cross, don't refuse the help. Ask God to bring people into your life that will help you bear. Ask God to remove people from your life who are piling on.

God listens. Always. He is the only One who can stop the world so you can get off. And into His arms.

CHAPTER 18

THE GRACELESS GOSPEL OF GUILT

Why have you despised the word of the Lord by doing evil in His sight? You have struck down Uriah the Hittite with the sword, have taken his wife to be your wife, and have killed him with the sword of the sons of Ammon. -- 2 Samuel 12:9

Those words spoken by Nathan at the request of the Lord to directly rebuke King David, forbearer of Jesus Christ, declared him guilty of lying, adultery and murder. A boatload of clearly-earned guilt for which he deserved to die.

Some people do. Die. Either from the punishment or from the burden of the guilt.

I think guilt may have killed my father. Not specific guilt for a specific action . . . but just the guilt of not being all he could have been, for not making more of himself, for not rising above, climbing higher, grasping the golden ring, for not meeting the expectations of others or even of himself. I used to think it was alcohol that killed him, but now I believe it may have been guilt. Not guilt *over* alcohol, but just plain old guilt. That "not-good-enough" guilt. Falling too short too often . . . and too witnessed. Each time he lowered his bar, the bar against which it was measured was raised. The vitality and hope of an adventurous boy swallowed up by the reality of a time-diminished lack of . . . hope. He just dimmed and flickered out.

The gospel of guilt: *From him who fails much, much failure is expected.*

I wish he had known that there is a cure for even a brokenness as consistent as his. Had I known then what I know now, I would have told him so . . . and perhaps he could have fought through it in this life and strode into eternity less-burdened . . . acknowledging that guilt is one of those odd gifts we give to the King. We hand Him our guilt; He sees our hidden hope and covers our guilt with His grace, so we too can see that hope.

How many men and women long to demonstrate a good soul, but never seem to make it onto the stage? Or they stride to the middle, stand in the glare of the spotlight and are booed into the silence before the first act begins? In the quietness of their minds, they say "I really am a good person. Really."

But the audience is ready for the next act.

On the flip side of the guilt-ridden are the guilt-riding. Instead of letting their own bad feelings get them down, they use those bad feelings to take others down. Such was my first stepfather. I'm not sure he ever really felt bad about anything he did . . . but he sure made you feel bad for him. He's the only person I ever knew who could awaken out of a drunken stupor and cuss about the boss who fired him for not showing up at work and the wife who had let him run out of cigarettes and whiskey. It was always someone else's fault that he was unable to have his bad habits and his good dreams in tandem. He would damn everyone around him and then demand a drink.

I wish I had known back then what I know now about guilt. And about grace. Guilt kills; grace restores.

If anyone should ever have succumbed to the debilitating misery of guilt, it should have been King David. He goes from the glory of killing Goliath and being hailed as a hero and warrior to the gritty grossness of using his ordained power to satisfy his own temptations by first spying on his neighbor's wife, committing adultery with her, making her pregnant, trying to disown the child by tricking the husband, and then, when all else fails, he puts the husband in a position to be killed. All to cover-up, not own-up, to his sin.

And we would say to David: "Boy . . . you are as guilty as sin." He was. It's enough to send you into hiding in a cave somewhere. David was no stranger to hiding in caves, having fled there before in fear. What does guilt produce but fear? And perhaps death.

And then there's grace. Grace brings you back out of the cave, if you accept it. If it can penetrate the walls of piled on guilt. If the warriors of the gospel of guilt don't stand outside the cave with swords of righteousness and slice grace down to a meaningless morsel and drive you back inside. That's not the armor of God they're wearing.

Some people equate a moral compass with a guilt compass. But they're not the same. With a guilt compass, the arrow points always downward and no matter how you turn it . . . it leads you no-where. The grace compass? Due north. Out of the cave. Down the highway. Back to the cross.

Guilt?

Grace?

I would rather be foolish or boring or simple or clumsy or slow or even ignorant . . . than guilty. I don't really want to be *any* of those things, of course, but have been at one time or another. I've been the fool, the bore, the clown, the simple-minded, slow-to-catch-on and the not-so-blissfully ignorant, all of which can lead to painful lessons . . . and moving on. Fool myself once, shame on me. Fool myself over and over again . . . guilt.

Now . . . don't think I believe there is no retribution for sin. David's path to redemption was not an easy one and we should have no expectations that ours will be. Consequences are . . . consequential. No matter how secret our sin, it is not beyond the full attention of God. Our consequences can be glaringly public.

> *Indeed you did it secretly, but I will do this thing before all Israel, and under the sun. Then David said to Nathan, "I have sinned against the Lord." And Nathan said to David, "The Lord also has taken away your sin; you shall not die. However, because by this deed you have given occasion to the enemies of the Lord to blaspheme, the child also that is born to you shall surely die." -- 2 Samuel 12:12-14*

The consequences of our sins often extend to others.

When we rise into grace, we may stand on legs with bloody knees and extend scraped palms. This is where the healing begins. Not in the dark recesses of the cave where we shiver in the dark, but in the light, where the pain begins to absorb the warmth of grace and we display our wounds and pray for healing. I just think that sometimes we look to the left and the right for someone to tell us how to get out of this pit of sorry guilt . . . and we need to look *up*. For correction and mercy and the courage to embrace grace.

> *He who conceals his sins does not prosper, but whoever confesses and renounces them finds mercy. -- Proverbs 28:13*

Yelling for mercy at the top of your lungs is a good thing. Just realize that God is not the only one listening. People have motivations, even if the stated goal is to assist in your restoration.

Some are *angry* because "you should have listened to me in the first place."

Some are *frustrated* because "you brought this on yourself."

Others are just *baffled* because "the right way was as plain as the nose on your face."

Others get a bit *puffed up* and want to set you on the path to righteousness so they can put another victory cup on their mantle.

Others want *revenge* because of the pain or the embarrassment your trip into guilt caused them personally.

Some are *striking back* out of their own pain because you betrayed them.

And then, there are some who just can't resist valuing *retribution* over restoration, making an example of you so others won't find themselves in your dismal state.

So . . . what happens to the downtrodden when he creeps out of the cave and gets hit with these misguided yet understandable motivations masquerading as "welcome back?"

Guilt. And a laundry list designed to work him back into the good graces of the condemners. Do we want "good graces" or true grace?

God's motivations are pure. He loves us and wants us back. He wants us to trust Him above all, cast aside all those things we think we know . . . and know Him first.

Trust in the Lord with all your heart and lean not on your own understanding; in all your ways acknowledge Him, and He will make your paths straight. -- Proverbs 3:5-6

Making the paths straight can involve working through some pretty serious consequences encountered as a result of our descent into the pit of guilt. But . . . He loves us so much He even walks with us through those consequences with the same unwavering love He used to coax us out of the cave. Cleaning up the mess we make is a community effort . . . communing with God, hanging close, keeping Him near, looking through His eyes to see the raging river of chaos as crossable and trusting those He brings into our lives to help carry us across.

He's called Emmanuel -- God *with* us -- for a reason. He knows our propensity to head back down the guilty road. And, if we insist on leading, He'll go there with us. But if we let Him lead, the road is straight to grace. We don't deserve His grace, and if we try to earn it, we'll just feel guilty because we can't do it right.

So . . am I saying that people are of no use to us as we pursue grace? Not at all. God works in the ways He wills . . . and sometimes He wills to use the most wonderful, grace-filled, straight-talking people in our lives to help us right ourselves, to stand on each side of us as we wobble along our way, to give stability and instruction, to sharpen our dullness back to a useful edge, to clean out the clutter, to sweep away the layers of deceitful dust.

> *For this reason I, Paul, the prisoner of Christ Jesus for the sake of you Gentiles -- if indeed you have heard of the stewardship of God's grace which was given to me for you; that by revelation there was made known to me the mystery, as I wrote before in brief. -- Ephesians 3:1-2*

God used Paul to extend His grace. We recognize the ones He wills to work in our lives when we realize their motivation matches His: love. And it is grace that allows us to accept the love of others and of God at the points in our lives when we feel our least-deserving. Wait on it. Don't rush headlong into the hands of the peddlers of guilt; wait for the enveloping arms of the purveyors of grace. Love will take your hand.

I received one piece of advice from the peddlers of guilt that has, in time, actually proven to be a bit of help: *"Now that you know it is wrong . . . just don't do it anymore."* That was not news to me; I already knew it was wrong. And, though it was a pretty callous comment, in the context of grace, it works. We have to know. And we have to stop. Unfortunately, the comment usually comes packaged like airplane model parts in a box without directions on how to put them together. Pieces of plastic. No clue what to glue to what. It's easier to put everything back in the box and tape down the lid.

If you think about it, *"now that you know what is wrong"* becomes *"now that you know what is right."* And *"don't"* becomes *"do."* God's Word unfolds like long-lost directions, with grace as the glue. The pieces fit together.

Feeling guilty does not set us free. Being equipped sets us free.

A GPS -- Global Positioning System -- will not get us back to the throne of grace. But a SPG – Salvation Per Grace -- will guide us there. It's easier to leave the cave when you know where you're going.

I don't know what you've done. I don't know who you hurt. I don't know who you betrayed. I don't know what all you did to cover up your trail, though I doubt that you killed someone in the cover-up, like David did. I do know that if your path to freedom from habitual sinning is blocked by piles of guilt, whether collected and placed there by you or carted in and arranged by others, it is not God's intent that you remain behind that wall.

> *Then David said to Nathan, "I have sinned against the Lord." And Nathan said to David, "The Lord also has taken away your sin; you shall not die." -- 2 Samuel 12:13*

David confessed. God forgave. He took the sins away and David was not guilty anymore. That is grace.

We can move beyond the mistakes we made and the choices we made and all the issues we created and the hurt we inflicted. Grace takes out the broken parts and creates something altogether new.

> *Therefore if anyone is in Christ, he is a new creature; the old things passed away; behold, new things have come. -- 2 Corinthians 5:17*

If you feel so guilty about what you've done and you don't think those things can pass away, let grace show it to you. It's true. New things come. God said so.

> *Therefore there is now no condemnation for those who are in Christ Jesus. -- Romans 8:1*

Believe it. I do now.

CHAPTER 19

It's Time for Letting Go

Therefore do not worry about tomorrow, for tomorrow will worry about itself. Each day has enough trouble of its own. -- Matthew 6:34

For the past thirty years or so, we've had this big, green, heavy antique piano in our living room. Over 100 years old, it has beautiful hand-carved woodwork, a massive overstrung scale, making it an upright grand piano with a rich rewarding tone. In our present house, it sits in a corner of the living-room like a massive monument to what might-have-been. Five children grew up around it and its keys remained in quiet rest, outside of a little clanky banging here and there. We dust it and we decorate it . . . green plants in the spring, a Nativity at Christmas time, family photos on occasion. But we never play it. It just takes up space and gets more antiquey.

It's not easy, I have found, to sell a *green* piano, judged immensely by its cover. I wonder where it spent the 80 years before we ended up with it. How many little ones had struggled with "Mary Had a Little Lamb?" How many piano masters had tinkled the ivories while dreamy-eyed listeners were swept away by the enchanting melody? Maybe it had found its way through an old honky-tonk, surrounded by drunks singing off key in search of harmony with fellow wanderers. I don't know where it has been or where it is going.

It's time to let it go.

I remember once in P.E. class back in about the 7th grade, during my geek-overload days, I would rather have been a solid antique green piano sitting like a brick in a dusty corner of the gymnasium than a gangly teen in too-short gym shorts next in line to swing on the ropes across an imaginary moat filled with alligators, as so colorfully described by the barking coach. I was to get a running start, grab a knot, swing as far as I could . . . and let go, my progress to be marked with masking tape on the cold hard floor. I ran, I grabbed, I held on until the swinging of the rope stopped and I hung deliciously above the hungry monsters in the moat.

It was way past time to let it go.

You might think I am possessive and clingy. I'm really not. I grew up familiar with loss and comfortably detached from most things and people. I don't have closets full of mementos, scrapbooks filled with pictures, high school yearbooks within easy access. Friends were good to have, especially on football Friday nights or at pizza parties and ice cream parlors. Family was good because of the familiarity and the higher possibility of fitting in somewhere, but there was always a little fear that someone would be moving on.

Gifts and souvenirs from little trips here and there were nice; they tied a person to a place and seemed to build some continuity, some sense that I was growing or going . . . somewhere. But, I rarely found anything much to hold on to. Things and people that hung around and truly became a part of my life seemed more to do so out of convenience and comfort. But, much as a favorite pillow eventually separates too much in the middle to provide much support for rest, all these things I would soon let go of . . . or find they had let go of me.

I have a paper star my daughter made me when she was very little. She wrote upon it "I love you." It has faded through the years and is hard to read, but I will always hang on to it. I have a 3-D spiky-haired portrait one of my sons sculpted completely out of hot glue. He would have tossed it. It's priceless to me. Another son drew Mickey Mouse with markers. It might as well be by Michelangelo because of its personal value. I have a pair of boots my second stepfather wore, his feet much smaller than mine. I can't wear them, but won't do away with them. An unfinished portrait of a grandson done by another son hangs in the hall and always will. I cherish an old VCR tape which shows another of my sons, barely-walking, on Christmas morning chewing through the peel of a banana because he is hungry and we are opening packages, unaware. These things, along with the millions of memories that bring a family through good and bad, are things of which I will never let go.

At this point in my life, though, I have reconciled that I have to let go of my children themselves, stepping aside from my own frantic and futile attempts to reconcile, trusting God to restore what He will, when He will, how He will. If He wills. This letting go is the hardest of all, and all who know me, know that I have fought vainly, wishful that the dam created by my sin could be removed and life could once again flow between us all. It would flow more freely now, not limited by the secrecy that once erected walls. We would live in truth; we would share in the goodness of change.

Letting go is in most cases a common-sense approach to moving on and growing to be more of what God intended. We pass over and under and through a lot of things that seem precious at the moment, perhaps up to the very moment that we let them go. And then we go. We turn the key for the last time in a door to a home that kept us safe. We hoist some things into the attic that used to surround us like walls of protection. We wave goodbye at airline gates or watch cars grow smaller as they drive down a familiar street en route to a different world and we stay behind. We lay a pet to rest. We lose on purpose a phone number or delete forever an e-mail address. We let go. Life is equal parts of letting go and taking in.

And then sometimes we just can't. Or so we believe. It would hurt too much to part with this or that, or him or her, to let it go. A grudge. A memory. A pain. A habit. A . . . *need?*

The things we refuse to let go of can form our personal prisons of pain and sorrow, blocking the freedom we so badly want; those of us who have been enslaved by sin. When we don't let go, we don't allow God to do His work of restoration in our lives. We exchange walking in trust for a common crutch and an acceptance of hobbling. We avoid growth for comfort. We cling to the familiar refrain and refuse to sing a new song. It hurts to get better. Too long in sin, like too long in the sun, leaves painful dead layers that have to be peeled away. Deliverance looks nice from a distance, but when it's time to embark on the journey itself, we settle for the comfort of our easy chair and our cozy cycles of chaos.

You are my hiding place; You will protect me from trouble and surround me with songs of deliverance. -- Psalm 32:7

The hardest letting is the letting go of some people in our lives. Truly some people are in our lives because they love us and want to help us be accountable on the new path we've chosen. Hold tight. Still, some people are in our lives because they remember the pain and they're seeking vengeance . . . a pound of flesh we just no longer have to give. Let them go . . . and hope they find God's grace and return some day in love so you can share your sincere regrets in a way they can receive them.

Sometimes letting go means prying out of your mind the memories that haunt you in your solitude. Rejections you felt long ago but put on a permanent re-wind in your mind. Abuse that clutters your heart and makes it hold back when you want to release it to love. Confusion that crowds in and chases clarity away, making you feel uncertain and unworthy of being redeemed. Guilt that grows stronger, fed by shame that you shine like a precious trophy on your mantle of self-destruction, gleaming from the polish of self-hatred.

Let go. Memories can fade and lose impact. Rejections can be replaced by accepting the love of others who are brave and able. Abuse can be forgiven. Yes . . . it really can. Confusion can be exchanged for the clarity of God's renewing of your mind . . . His ability to show you who He created you to be. Guilt and shame can succumb to the power of confession and repentance. The mantle of self-destruction can be disassembled and the trophies crushed beneath the weight of God's reconstruction of the soul and heart and mind.

But . . . not unless we let go. Let go of all these things that make up our world, these things we conform ourselves to, these things which morph into a hard mold out of which we cannot seem to break.

How?

Take God at His word.

Do not conform any longer to the pattern of this world, but be transformed by the renewing of your mind. Then you will be able to test and prove what God's will is—His good, pleasing and perfect will. -- Romans 12:2.

I am so ready to test God's will. I've tested mine. I don't approve. My self-will is not "good, pleasing and perfect." I ache to be transformed.

I need to let it go.

I'm afraid I've allowed myself to sit in the corner like an underplayed piano, hiding the melody, waiting for someone to fold back the keyboard cover and discover the music inside. A lot of time passes and a lot of dust collects while we hold on to what we were instead of becoming what we are. Priceless.

There is some sorrow in letting go, but there is greater joy in letting God. There is emptiness in casting out, but there is fullness in God's generous restoration.

Like me, you can do a personal inventory. In stillness and receptiveness before God, the closets open and the deceptive precious things come out of the dark. Let them go. Give them up. Find the intended melody hidden beneath the discord in your soul.

It's time for letting go.

CHAPTER 20

LEAVING THE LAND OF LOOKING BACK

He wants to get his life together; he knows there's something more,
If he can leave the land of Looking Back and the tempting treasures stored.
But in every trip through Looking Back are things he can't ignore,
And the dust and decay of yesterday are his lookin' back reward.

Take this key; give Me yours; We're going out that door.
Leave the halls and constant falls; use this map to stay on track.
Take My hand, lean on Me; give Me yours, there is more,
Than the dust and decay of the wandering way
through the Land of Looking Back.

The man who travels through Looking Back seems determined to lose his way
With the key in his pocket and the map in his
mind but a question in his soul.
Yet the Guide who is able, the One who is
worthy, could end this constant stray.
The arm on his shoulder, the hand on his heart; He's already paid his toll.

The key the man carries just makes it so easy for
Looking Back to look like home.
And the map in his mind makes the journey
so easy there's no reason not to go.
For the home is so cozy, the shadows so cool, it's a comfortable route to roam,
But the arm on his shoulder and the hand on
his heart is faithfully telling him no.

Take this key; give Me yours; We're going out that door.
Leave the halls and constant falls; Here's a map to stay on track.

Take My hand, lean on Me; give Me yours, there is more
Than the dust and decay of the wandering way
through the Land of Looking Back.

The Looking Back man looks out and looks in;
He's not looking up and praying,
The windows are cracked and the door dark
and black, as beckoning as before.
With a trembling hand, he locks the drawer
where the pain of his past is laying,
With a glance back behind and a turn to the
front, he looks for a different door.

In his hand is a key, not rusted or bent, to a door at the end of the hall.
New and unbroken, finished out with fresh paint, a window lets in the light.
With new key in hand, but the map in his
mind still daring the walker to stall,
He takes the arm of the One who has promised forever to end his fight.

Take My will; give Me yours; We're going out that door.
Leave the halls and the falls; Here's a map; there's the track.
Leave the dust and decay, let Me clean and restore,
When we go through that door, there's no going
back to the land of Looking Back.

-- Thom Hunter

When I was in my final days of elementary school, I would travel each morning and afternoon through the neighborhoods of Houston on a crowded school bus, sitting silently by a window, surrounded by laughing and shouting classmates . . . and I would study the yards of the homes we passed. Through familiarity, the neighborhoods would sort into the dids and didn'ts. Those who mowed regularly and edged and trimmed and those who didn't. Those who cleared the clutter and those who kept the clutter around them like comfort. With only a passing glance, it would have been just a neighborhood, but viewing each side of the street once a day . . . it distinguished itself into a long row of families in various stages of discipline or disarray.

I became familiar, most of all, with the "yard art." The cedar wheelbarrow planters . . . the bird baths . . . and the wishing wells. Even these would demonstrate the conditions of their owners. Some planters were re-finished regularly and ablaze with colorful pansies and begonias; others were fading away and tilting forward under the weight of dying weeds and branches that had fallen from untrimmed trees. Some bird baths were dusty and dry; others overflowed with cool clear water in which birds ducked and dived or sat on the side and shared their melodies.

The wishing wells? They weren't "wells" at all of course, but just painted planks of boards and little shingled roofs assembled in garages by men with a little spare time to think while creating a gift for their wives from tools and saws collected over the years of Fathers' Days. They had followed the directions and finished the project. Some of the wells -- those of the dids -- were painted and had little buckets on ropes that went no-where but seemed like they would. The others -- those of the didn'ts -- faded and leaned and developed rotting spots and cracks and were surrounded by tall grass.

I don't think, in the fifth grade, that I considered whether the conditions of the ornaments in the yards reflected anything about the people behind the doors of the homes. I lived in an apartment and our yard art was limited to a wind chime in the spring and summer and a Christmas wreath in winter, a golden thing made from old IBM punch cards, folded and spray-painted and decorated with plastic berries. Neither the chime nor the wreath said much to anyone about what went on behind the door.

I remember when one of Oklahoma's frequent tornadoes passed through a couple of miles away and took direct aim on a wishing well I have driven past a thousand times. The owner of the home had, the morning after, run about his yard and picked up all the broken boards and scattered shingles, the frayed rope and the little bucket and piled it in his yard. A shrine to all the wishes blown away by the wayward and uncaring wind? A dead circle in the yard revealed the hard dirt and discolored Bermuda grass that had been the bottom of the "well," a place where wishes would have landed with a thud.

Whatever wishes had been cast into the well were about as effective as those we toss with our coins into fountains in the park, or sling into the night sky to welcome the first star we see, or silently offer before we blow out the candles on our cake.

Wishing wells are not a fad; they transcend generations. As long as wives are wishing, men will be building wells. While similar to hoping and praying, so many of our wishes are backward-aimed. I *wish* this had not happened. I *wish* this had. Our looking-back puts brakes on our moving forward. Our defective past drowns our effective future. Our didn'ts disable our dos.

Sometimes we think we want it like it was back then because it was easier. Deception provides a cushion from the truth. For the truth is that in almost all cases, the plans He has laid out for us are so much better than the ones we carved through the wilderness when we made our own way. It just looks better when we look back because at least we recognize it. Kind of like that comfortable recliner in a living room that we would recognize as a total mess in someone else's home. It fits and we like it, but it probably needs to be tossed.

> *By the time Lot reached Zoar, the sun had risen over the land. Then the Lord rained down burning sulfur on Sodom and Gomorrah -- from the Lord out of the heavens. Thus He overthrew those cities and the entire plain, including all those living in the cities -- and also the vegetation in the land. But Lot's wife looked back, and she became a pillar of salt. -- Genesis 19:23-26*

Yikes. Salt? Longing for the Land of Looking Back, she paused and becomes a pillar and then, due to those wayward winds again, a spreading of particles on the plains.

I think it must really frustrate God when He gives us new plans and we keep looking back in yearning. That is, if God becomes frustrated. After all, He is in control. But surely He shakes his head when we toss a penny whimsically in a wishing well instead of casting all our cares in prayer.

I met with my oldest son in hopes of restoring a relationship destroyed by my deception. We shared lunch and some silence punctuated by a pinch of promise and a small heaping of hope. But . . . it was the looking back that hurt.

"I wish things weren't as they were."

That's what he said before parting. I wish I did not wonder what he meant. I wish he had not tangled all of life into this curious mixture of tenses, a mishmash of past and present. What does it mean: "I wish things weren't as they were?" I'm caught up first in the impotency of wishes. Strike that word altogether. Then there is the "weren't." That's the looking back. Add the "were," but say it with the look of present tense in the eyes and the small heaping of hope is whisked off the table like a few scattered grains of spilled salt.

Looking back. We look back and we say because it was, it is. Why not say. . . "I pray that things aren't as they were." Take away the wish . . .

adjust the tense . . . and fate becomes faith. Looking back becomes moving forward. Old habits become foreign to new creatures.

> *Therefore, if anyone is in Christ, he is a new creation; the old has gone, the new has come! All this is from God, who reconciled us to Himself through Christ and gave us the ministry of reconciliation: that God was reconciling the world to Himself in Christ, not counting men's sins against them. -- 2 Corinthians 5:17-19*

Why is it that some of the most oft-quoted verses are given such short-shrift in belief? That verse is not just a little heaping of hope. It says "anyone." It says "new." It says it is "from God." It says "reconciled." It says "not counting men's sins against them." And it says it is all about Christ.

You mean . . . it's not about me? It's not about what I did? Didn't?

No. It is about Christ.

You mean it's not about going back and cleaning up all the messes? Putting the wishing well back together? Planting the wheelbarrow with pretty flowers?

No. It's about Christ.

> *He who was seated on the throne said, "I am making everything new!" Then He said, "Write this down, for these words are trustworthy and true." He said to me: "It is done. I am the Alpha and the Omega, the Beginning and the End. To him who is thirsty I will give to drink without cost from the spring of the water of life. He who overcomes will inherit all this, and I will be his God and he will be My son." -- Revelation 21:5-7*

Everything?

Drink without cost?

Inherit through overcoming?

His son?

So . . . it's not all about me . . . but it *is* all about me. At least all about His love for me and His desire for me to overcome and be His son. All for His glory.

I know we have to look back for the purpose of confessing what we've done and reconciling what was done to us, so we can repent of what we did and what we did in response to what someone did in response to what we did. But, if all we do is look back, we aren't confessing; we're not repenting and we're surely not overcoming. And we find ourselves wishing "things weren't as they were," instead of rejoicing that things are as they are.

Learning from the past is good. But just like I never again want to be a fifth grader cruising Houston neighborhoods on a crowded yellow bus . . . I don't want to cruise the Land of Looking Back. It is a land filled with broken cedar wheelbarrows, decaying wishing wells and drought-stricken songless birdbaths. The yard art in the Land of Looking Back succumbed long ago to the wicked weeds of remembered deeds.

One of the hardest things to resist is sticking a thumb out in the wind when those around us whiz by on their way to take another trip through our Looking Back. We may not be able to convince them to put down the maps and cancel the tour, but we don't have to go along or volunteer to serve as the guide. We can wish -- strike that -- pray that one of these days they will realize we've moved.

The old has gone.

CHAPTER 21

THE STRUGGLER HAS MANY FACES

I got a better picture of who we're meant to be
When God revealed your soul to me.
Sometimes I wonder why we strive
Until I see you so alive.

The way you search, the way you seek
Gives me more than just a peek.
Because in you I begin to see
A part of what God can do in me.

The pain, the joy wrapped up in you
The things you share that you've been through
Remind me Christ is always there
No pain, no loss beyond His care.

Thank you for the life you live
Thank you for the hope you give.
You thought you shared your words with me,
But God revealed your soul, you see.

-- Thom Hunter

If my personal life could divide neatly into decades, like we do with our cultural countdowns -- the '50s, the '60s, the '70s, the '80s, the '90s, the whatevers, the '10s -- I would have to say the 05s and beyond have been my period of moving forward.

Moving forward does not mean we leave all of everything behind. It means we toss aside the baggage that has weighed us down, stopped us in our tracks, set us on distracting detours . . . the junk that clutters the attic . . . the weeds that obscure the sidewalk . . . the shag carpet . . . the broken tools in the garage . . . the old letters in the box that spell out in detail the errors of the past.

Lightened up, we get to keep those good snapshots, meaningful memories and bright moments when we were on the track, before we somehow left the rails. And though we can move forward together, we don't have to come from the same place; we just have to have the same source of energy.

Or . . . as Bob Hamp, director of Freedom Ministries, says, we have to realize that God is always seeking to restore the factory settings. To make us like new again.

Despite -- or maybe because of -- the cultural push to normalize homosexuality, I believe the perspective of Christians on the reality of sexual brokenness has matured, providing greater hope for me and for others. Perhaps it is in the clarity of statements such as "The opposite of homosexuality is not heterosexuality; it is holiness," being repeated by the leaders of organizations like Exodus International. Or perhaps it is the reminder, again from Exodus, that "freedom is not the absence of struggle, but instead is knowing that the struggle is not in vain."

If strugglers then, focus more on their holiness than on their sexuality, their sexual temptations become less a wallowing in guilt and more a sacrifice to holiness.

Steve Payton, pastor of Stonegate Church in Midland, Texas, offers hope to strugglers: "God will only let his child run for so long and then He will draw you back." Granted, sometimes he draws us back out of a pretty deep ditch, enabling us to drop the tool with which we are digging ourselves in deeper.

And while so many for so long have made it so clear that I have sinned, Payton has a clarifying definition: "Sin is me believing I can get on my own something better than what God is giving me." How many times have I praised God's loving generosity with one hand and longed for self-satisfaction with the other?

Uhh . . . sin.

More than anything, Christians need clarity in this battle, whether they are the ones who struggle or they are the ones who love the struggler. I wish every pastor in the country -- make that the world -- could hear former Exodus International President Joe Dallas explain the differences between homosexual orientation, identity, and behavior.

Orientation is involuntary, discovered.

Behavior is what we do with that discovery via our free will.

Identity is what is sometimes foisted on us, sometimes embraced, but not who we really are. Not in God's created intent, but only in our fallen nature.

Say it's so Joe: "To be loved by God and approved by God are two different things." How many times have I felt God's love even in an unapproved state? And, if I had not felt that love when I could find none of my own for myself, and found it in scant supply in the community, how could I have yearned to turn?

The enduring love of God braces those who are ever in danger of falling. The personal thread of endurance can run alongside the reality of the strong chord of God's grace.

But . . . what is most valuable to me when I look at fellow strugglers? Their resolve. The open hearts and exposed souls seeking holiness and pouring their energies into pleasing God above themselves. They are the ones who provide fuel for my own endurance because they are on the painful road to freedom for themselves or those they love. We are not alone on this journey. We gain courage and take comfort from fellow travelers.

Like Elena, whose smile expresses the soul of an encourager. Elena does not struggle with sexual brokenness, but her desire is to learn about and understand the trapping temptations of a close friend of hers, so she can listen to her friend with a knowledgeable mind and a clearer heart. Elena will walk further now, and her friend will be blessed. God uses pure-hearted servants like Elena.

Or, like James and Jessica . . . a young couple coming to terms with James' struggle with homosexuality, which is a challenge for them both . . . yes . . . for them both. Jessica is by his side, loving him, encouraging him, listening with him, talking with him, walking with him. Learning. Yearning. Sharing. Caring. Having faith . . . together.

And Matthew, alone on a sad journey, enduring the solitude that often comes before the joy of healing tips the scales. Matthew's wife is pregnant with their first child . . . but she has decided to divorce him because of his struggle with homosexuality. Matthew displays the hopeful but hurting persona of the trodden down who forces himself to look up. He wants to be free; he hopes to hold on to the love of his life by surrendering the burden of his sin.

I know a young man who is clearly in pursuit of truth and anxious to understand and confront his unwanted sexual attraction to men. He describes his enslavement to temptation as suffocation and yearns to breathe new air, the air of grace, to refresh lungs exhausted by the fear of living forever outside of God's intent. He wants to move forward.

Hope is all around, such as in the lives of a young pastor and his wife. The pastor's long-held and deeply-hidden secret cost him his church. Now healed and open and transparent, he shares with others the freedom he has found in the healing that only comes through persistent leaning on the arms of Christ. Despite having been restored to the ministry and again pastoring a church, he feels the call to leave it and become a "missionary" to the hopeful hurting in his midst, his wife by his side. His battle has given him a deep level of trust in the Lord, despite the rejection that lingers from those who once saw him as an unredeemable something else. From hurting to healed to called. He is anxious to share openly what many bury under the unnecessary weight of sin and guilt. He knows such hiding reflects not the intentions of God, but the inflictions of man.

Christian families all over the world confront the issues of the various forms of sexual brokenness . . . even if their church families are unaware or ill-equipped. Help is on the way, through people like Ted and Jan Schneider, directors of About H.O.P.E.—Heal Our Pain El Shaddai.

Ted and Jan found themselves stunned years ago when their son revealed to them that he considered himself to be gay. They were not prepared; they knew not where to go or how to react. They loved their son; they knew God's word. Neither of those positions changed as the years passed and they endured in love. With tears, Jan told of the day when they received the call that their son had been killed in a car accident; their loss immeasurable; their hearts broken. And from this, Jan cried out to God to "please not let this pain be wasted." God hears when the broken-hearted faithfully cry out. Their ministry was born to help the families and friends of those involved in the homosexual lifestyle know how to live and breathe and love, to help parents understand and support through truthful compassion not tainted by compromise.

From our losses He builds bridges.

I need bridges.

In a world of ever-louder clanging confusion in the clash between culture and the church in this seemingly endless battle that has gripped the lives of so many and of those who love them, the testimonies of those who have experienced God's grace are bringing clarity and hope. In worship and prayer, in study and sharing, in listening and in releasing, the struggler finds a security in the overwhelming evidence that God is indeed who He says He is and we are indeed who He says we are: His beloved.

Strugglers can face the battle better-armed, on stronger legs with clearer minds and healing hearts, with comfort and acceptance . . . and an openness to God based on a promise that God really . . . *really* knows us . . . and heals our broken hearts.

> *I praise you because I am fearfully and wonderfully made; Your works are wonderful, I know that full well. My frame was not hidden from You when I was made in the secret place. When I was woven together in the depths of the earth, Your eyes saw my unformed body. All the days ordained for me were written in Your book before one of them came to be. -- Psalm 139:14-16*

> *Search me, O God, and know my heart; test me and know my anxious thoughts. -- Psalm 139:23*

Perhaps the most difficult thing in seeing others who strive to overcome, but lack support, is to look around and wonder . . . why? Why, in a world of sin, is this sin so over-valued, as if it were something God has not equipped His church to handle in truth and compassion? It is as if we think God's ability to act is based on our ability to comprehend.

But as Kathy Koch, founder of Celebrate Kids, Inc., says: "God gives us promises; not explanations."

> *"But I will restore you to health and heal your wounds," declares the Lord, "because you are called an outcast, Zion for whom no one cares." -- Jeremiah 30:17*

God does heal our wounds, and He does use His people to do it. People like my wife. Lisa opened her eyes instead of closing her mind, extended the boundaries of her heart and placed her trust in Him above all others. God uses those who love us as powerful weapons in the struggle

There is a great blessing when we move forward under the power of the Holy Spirit, with believers by our side. That blessing is multiplied when we extend a hand and bring others along with us.

CHAPTER 22

The Heartache of an Echo

Where is God? ...Go to Him when your need is desperate, when all other help is vain, and what do you find? A door slammed in your face, and a sound of bolting and double-bolting on the inside. After that, silence.

— C.S. Lewis, after the death of his wife.

My grandfather was a man of few words. At least he was to me. I was often just an intrusive little boy who always forgot to not slam the screen door when running in and out. I'd yell out an "I'm sorry" as I bounded down the porch steps or down the hall. Paw-Paw, sitting at a card table playing Solitaire, would usually just make a grunting noise in return, not looking up from the cards, though once I paused and saw him smile. That told me a lot more than the grunt.

I regret now that I was always dashing in and out and passing his table with little thought. He was so accessible, but for some reason I felt he would have little to say, not a lot in common, and might want me to linger longer than I wanted to. So, I dashed and slammed. What was so much more important? Hide-and-seek with the now-forgotten neighborhood kids in our connecting yards? A comic book down the hall that needed reading?

I wonder if the slamming door echoed in the emptiness of the room in which he often sat alone playing his cards or eating syrup on bread? How long did the smile stay on his face?

I do know that my grandfather was not a man of few words with everyone. He helped my older brother assemble a motorcycle. That takes more than a grunt. And I do remember him putting some pretty stern and loud polish on a few words here and there . . . again usually spoken to my brother, often from the front porch as the motorcycle disappeared down the street. Probably sent the neighbor kids into a deeper form of hide-and seek.

I wouldn't necessarily say Paw-Paw had a way with words, seeing as how he somehow gave my grandmother the nickname "Bump," a term of endearment she endured until his death and probably repeated in her peaceful thoughts until her own.

What words would he have had for me had I listened? Would I have had a nickname? What might Paw-Paw have wanted to hear had I slowed and sat a moment at the table? Maybe he was much more interested in me than I thought. I believe he was. Maybe he would have said more if I had sought more. I believe he would have.

I never picture God as a grandfather, puttering around in the garage for spare parts to make this or that work again. He doesn't tinker. He ticked the first tick and knows all and sees all and hears all . . . but sometimes I think He plays a little Solitaire.

How about Hearts instead, God? Deal me in.

I know that God is omni-present; but it seems every now and then He is omni-absent. The sign on the door says "Gone Fishing," the lights are out, the doorbell dings in an empty room, the No Vacancy sign is on . . . drive on down the road . . . alone. Yes, I know that is not true; He never leaves me; He never leaves you. Even as I sit here and write questions about His absence, He knows each keystroke in advance. But . . . will He keep me from misspelling? Bad grammar? No.

Wasn't He there, in the Garden of Eden, right *after* Adam and Eve's encounter with the serpent? His Word says God came walking up in the cool of the day. Surely He was also there in the heat of the moment. Yet He didn't clear his throat and wag his finger and say "Ummm . . . Eve, no, no, no." So Eve did, did, did and we've been done for since.

God was oddly silent and then clearly loud.

I'll admit that it bothers me a bit to know that God was with me before I slipped and, with all the power of the universe, watched me tumble, twist and turn on the way down, hit the bottom with a gut-wrenching and bone-jarring thud . . . and then He comes out in the cool of the day as if He had not seen it all happen. Is He really a "what's up?" God?

No.

Wait for the Lord. Be strong and let your heart take courage. Yes, wait for the Lord. -- Psalm 27:14

110

But I don't want to wait. I want to act. I want to meet a . . . need? I *want!*

How many of us, when we are dialing a number we shouldn't know; turning into an area we shouldn't go, logging on to a website we shouldn't see, acting like someone we shouldn't be . . . say to ourselves: "Wait . . . let me ask God about this?"

It's easy to say He's not speaking when we're not pausing. It's pure spiritual finger-pointing to say He's not responding when we're not reflecting.

I think sometimes we think we might prefer a "No . . . No . . . No . . ." wagging-a-warning-finger God. And we would, of course, gently lay down our pride, sweep aside our defiance, thank Him profusely for keeping us from falling, pledge our undying trust and obey without question. Or perhaps we would eat of the fruit; gain the knowledge we do not need; satisfy the glutton side of our spirit and waddle into our all-too-familiar rescue me mode.

Fact of the matter is, God does wag a "No . . . No. . . No. . . " finger in our faces. We just ignore it and say we didn't hear Him. Are we actually expecting God to sit by our bedside and read His Word aloud to us at night?

> *My son, do not forget My teaching, but keep My commands in your heart, for they will prolong your life many years and bring you prosperity. Let love and faithfulness never leave you; bind them around your neck; write them on the tablet of your heart. Then you will win favor and a good name in the sight of God and man. Trust in the Lord with all your heart and lean not on your own understanding; in all your ways acknowledge Him, and He will make your paths straight. Do not be wise in your own eyes; fear the Lord and shun evil. -- Proverbs 3:1-7*

OK . . . I'll do that. But . . . remind me. Okay, God? I just might forget.

Oops . . . that was how the verse began: "do not forget." And it asks me to "keep." Keep what? Those commands I so easily tossed to lighten the load as I traveled down the me-want road. And . . . oh yeah . . . He wanted me to write "love and faithfulness" on the tablet of my heart. But . . . that's *my* heart. There's not much writing room left; I've done a lot of scribbling and mark-outs through the years trying to satisfy the longings of my heart.

Of course then He wants me to trust. Trust? Lust? Tough choices we face in this life. He says if I trust Him instead of myself . . . he will take all those crooked detours, jagged fault lines, dangerous drop-offs, and impossible mountains . . . those cliffs . . . out of my path and make it "straight." We're not talking sexual semantics here . . . we're talking direction . . . which can certainly lead to some serious sexual semantics.

So what else does this "silent" God, who has looked up at me as I once again slammed a door in haste, have to say? He says for me to not "be wise in my own eyes." Who knew that the pursuit of wisdom could be so dangerous? Well . . . Eve, I guess, in retrospect. Adam, too. And, oh yes, the serpent. But he knew it all along. Surely God doesn't want me to just be stupid? I'd get into so much trouble. Oh . . . yeah. That.

> *For the foolishness of God is wiser than man's wisdom, and the weakness*
> *of God is stronger than man's strength. -- I Corinthians 1:25*

I remember driving out onto a lonely hill at the edge of the town I grew up in, seeing the lights in the distance and thinking of each of them as a porch light in a home where everything was right and good, every body tucked in for the night, every heart satisfied, every mind at rest, every soul at peace.

Lacking the courage to call out to God, I repeated instead within my mind what all was not right with my world . . . my home . . . my heart . . . my soul . . . my peace. And those words echoed within the emptiness . . . and brought me heartache. I had come to the hill alone . . . and remained there alone . . . and departed alone. My choice.

We may come to the garden alone . . . but we shouldn't leave that way. He is so accessible, but He might want us to linger a little longer than we want to. So, we dash and slam. "Oops . . . sorry."

What must really be difficult for God -- if anything could ever so be labeled -- is to hear the echoes of His own Word as it descends into our valleys and reverberates against the emptiness we feel as we seek to satisfy ourselves with increasing self-absorption. We want to move that mountain, cross that valley, swim that ocean . . . and then . . . when totally satiated, cry out "Where were you, God?"

With you.

The heartache of His echo.

I know sometimes it seems that we are all alone in whatever battle has worked to separate us from His love, whatever temptation has tattered our goodness, whatever sin has led to our shunning. But we are never alone. We would not, could not, will not be alone.

Having trouble finding your own way out of your mess? Tempted to blame God, declaring Him absorbed in some sort of Solitaire while you slowly slip away?

Maybe, in some small way, God really is like Paw-Paw. Maybe I would hear more than a grunt; see more than a passing smile . . . if I would open a few doors here and there instead of slamming them as I proceed to and fro on my own. Maybe if I played a little less hide-and-seek, put away the comics -- the pursuit of happiness as defined by culture -- and paused at the table, talked to Him, listened to Him, pulled out the chair, sat down . . . and waited.

Like He asked me to do in the first place. Remember?

Wait for the Lord. Be strong and let your heart take courage. Yes, wait for the Lord. -- Psalm 27:14

You know, that's what I always wanted: to be strong, to have courage. And He said I could. If I would wait for Him. I bet that was a resounding echo.

I do love God. And, with God, Solitaire is a team sport. One heart.

Next time you find yourself feeling the pain of self-induced pity at your pitiful plight of weakness in the face of temptation, remember: Wait. Be strong. Take courage. Wait.

We don't do that very well, do we? Waiting. Waiting on the Lord. Want . . . wait. A choice that can lead us into a celebration of conversation or a heartache of echoes, purpose or pain, oneness or aloneness. Victory or defeat. Restoration or repetition. A straight path or an endless cycle.

God is never silent. He spoke every answer in advance of every question.

CHAPTER 23

IF YOU'RE GOING THROUGH HELL, DON'T STOP AT THE GIFT SHOP

For a man's ways are in full view of the LORD, and He examines all his paths. The evil deeds of a wicked man ensnare him; the cords of his sin hold him fast. He will die for lack of discipline, led astray by his own great folly. -- Proverbs 5: 21-23

We are often visited here at our home by large black birds which walk around the yard pulling bugs from the grass as they sneak their way toward the dog food bowl, the real prize. Our two big black dogs lay sleeping, but often with one eye open so they can pounce at the birds just inches shy of the bowl. The birds flee to a nearby tree, then drop to the ground and begin again their determined march as soon as the dogs relax. The dogs keep watch and pounce again, but occasionally they doze off completely and the persistent birds escape with their Purina prize. The cycle repeats and no one really wins, but the dogs and birds grow comfortable in the familiarity of the battle. Are they enemies? Are they adversaries? Or are they just at play at the sport of life? I am mainly an observer from my office window, drawn into this cycle, though perhaps a bit of an enabler, since I do buy the food in 50-pound bags. I am amused by the endless cycle.

When I think of hell, I think of endless cycles . . . unrealized hope punched to breathless despair, a prize always extended, but guarded by the hounds of hell and their "you never will" growls. Sneaking and fleeing, pouncing and preying . . . over and over with the same results. And everything is black, determined to absorb and defeat any stray impulse of light. Desires to overcome acquiesce to a simple acceptance of survival. What should have been becomes what will never be. Hope rests on the bottom of a raging sea churning like a vast whirlpool, holding it down, burying it deeper beneath the silt of life.

Fortunately, I rarely think of hell . . . other than to acknowledge its existence and the truth that God, in His love for me and as proof of His excellent greatness, provides a way to never really know what hell is like. But, unfortunately, the proverbial "hell on earth" is all-too familiar to many. It varies in its intensity, from a camouflaged pool of quicksand to a raging whirlpool itself, pulling us down, sapping all our energy to grasp for one more breath, leaving us dazed to ask ourselves . . . "how did I get here?"

When I was young, my mother took us -- her trusting little children -- to the drive-in movie to see *The Birds*. I never really understood it that well. Melanie, a pretty woman, buys a couple of beautiful birds, jets across to Bodega Bay wearing high heels in a speed boat, raises everyone's suspicions and pretty soon all the big black birds on the island start swirling around, attacking kids on the playground, plucking out the eyes of the plucky school teacher and generally wreaking complete havoc on the pretty little town. The pretty woman goes kooky.

My mother took us to see *The Birds* on a dark stormy night and we rushed home in the thunder and lightning and I lay awake fearing my eyes would be plucked out. Thanks, Mom. Nothing from Disney was showing?

If all's well that ends well, it's nice to know that the school teacher was reincarnated as Bob Newhart's wife in a happy sitcom years later and Bodega Bay thrives today as a world-class resort and bird-watcher's dream. Melanie? I think she lived out her life flailing her arms, but with a perfectly-coiffed honey-colored beehive hairdo.

But . . . all does not always end well for the countless people caught up in the various cycles they would describe as their personal hell. Those voracious addictions that creep in on little bird legs and then come swooping back with powerful black wings and menacing beaks to peck away the dignity and the peace that preceded the addictions to pornography and seduction and lust. Some of the addictions arose from great inner emptiness, a desire to be loved and touched and valued; a desire that perverts itself into being used and using, a wandering that leads to being ever unfulfilled. And the question the wanderer has, even in the uncertainty of where he is at any given moment: "how did I get here?"

There is a way that seems right to a man, but in the end it leads to death. -- Proverbs 16:25

In my travels through the desert of addiction, I spent too much time wishing for sympathy. I wanted those who did not understand to at least stand. I wanted those who were hurt to also see *my* pain. I wanted those who judged to set aside the robes and gavels and extend a hand of mercy. I wanted those who shunned to support. I wanted those who ran away to walk beside. I wanted those who jeered to cheer. I wanted those who cringed to cry with me. I wanted those who pointed fingers to offer a hand. I wanted . . . .

And some did. There are those who take on whirlpools.

But not many.

So . . . we learn that hell on earth is a nightmarish vacation spot of solitude and we make the best of it. We shop as we travel through, sampling a bit of the goodies, trying to determine if this might be a place to retire to someday. If we don't pace ourselves, we may shop until we drop.

First Stop: Defensiveness Department. Here we find excuses carefully laid out for every size and fashion. And they fit. They really do. For in many cases, these addictions we bear truly are not our fault at all. Naysayers can nay all they want, but it is true that the abused are skewed and the bullied are blunted and the left-behind are left-resigned to be less than those who were nurtured and protected and guided.

Second Stop: The Settlement Sale. Here we find on display the limitations and labels that tell us we never have been and never will be as whole as everyone else, so we may as well adjust to our limitations and do the best we can. We spend a little time in the alterations department and accept our limitations, telling others they may as well accept us as we are because we cannot be more.

Third Stop: The Makeup Counter. If we cannot escape our flaws, we find what we need to cover them. Deep discounts are available here for the double-life. We go throughout our day with a painted on smile and an inner voice behind our too-bright eyes: "if you only knew me as I really am."

Fourth Stop: Desperation Discounts. This is the bargain basement. These clothes have been tried on and rejected so often that they're on the verge of being rendered into rags. Who cares? They're cheap. No one looks at me anymore anyway. We end up in the basement when we have determined that it doesn't really matter anymore what we do or what we say or what persona we project. Everyone's mind is made up and our label is affixed. We're as worthless as the deepest of the deep discounts.

That's what sexual brokenness does. It drops you to your lowest inner denominator. And it feels like hell. The traveling businessman who makes a deal in the afternoon and scarcely finds time for dinner because porn is available in the hotel room. The same-sex attraction struggler who suffocates in the silence of his or her living room and finds a reason to go out and search for sound . . . and sex. The lonely married man or woman who moves from sex partner to sex partner in search of . . . what? . . . understanding . . . comfort . . . completion . . . power . . . calling it pleasure . . . declaring it deserved? The ones addicted to masturbation because their satisfaction seems bound up in fantasy now. The real world has become distant and just doesn't do it anymore.

They're cruising hell, collecting coupons and sifting through the bargain basement all along the way. And the aisles are crowded, though the only way they can handle their own despair is to deny what they see in others pushing the baskets along beside them. "Hey . . . we must be okay. After all, here we all are, just out shopping."

Did anyone happen to notice it's awfully dark in there? You can scarcely see to make your best selections. It's all running together into a grab and go. Anyone see the switch?

> *God saw that the **light** was good, and He separated the **light** from the darkness. -- Genesis 1:4*

> *Even in darkness **light** dawns for the upright, for the gracious and compassionate and righteous man. -- Psalm 112:4*

> *Your word is a lamp to my feet and a **light** for my path. -- Psalm 119:105*

> *Who among you fears the Lord and obeys the word of His servant? Let him who walks in the dark, who has no **light**, trust in the name of the Lord and rely on his God. -- Isaiah 50:10*

> *The people living in darkness have seen a great **light**; on those living in the land of the shadow of death a **light** has dawned. -- Matthew 4:16*

*When Jesus spoke again to the people, He said, "I am the **light** of the world. Whoever follows Me will never walk in darkness, but will have the **light** of life." -- John 8:12*

Have you ever toured a cavern or traveled down into a vast cave? It was dark and cold and mysterious and dangerous, filled with potential to slip or fall and slide into the dark abyss. But . . . in front of you was a guide, with a light. Sure, you had the responsibility to keep one foot in front of the other, to follow the path, to not wander into the uncharted detours. But, in front of you the light persisted and moved forward and eventually you would emerge into the awesome, almost unbearable brightness of the daylight sun.

If you looked back behind you into the deep dark hole, you found yourself thinking "Thank God for the guide. I could have been stuck in there forever."

For those of you who are wandering in the darkness of addiction and brokenness, turn away from the deep discounts of discarded merchandise and look for the light. Are you asking someone to show you the way out? It's okay to want people to walk with us, to support us, to pray for us, to stand with us, to forgive us, but only One will guide the way out. The One who holds the light and knows the way.

*Jesus answered, "I am the **way** and the **truth** and the **life**. No one comes to the Father except through Me." -- John 14:6.*

And it's free.

CHAPTER 24

JESUS WASN'T HOME IN TIME FOR DINNER

How can you say to your brother, 'Brother, let me take the speck out of your eye,' when you yourself fail to see the plank in your own eye? You hypocrite, first take the plank out of your eye, and then you will see clearly to remove the speck from your brother's eye. – Luke 6:42

Do you ever wake up in the middle of the night and do a life review? In that rear-view mirror of reclining restlessness, all the wrong turns of the past seem to paint a clear direction to the present. That retrospective road map can be painfully revealing.

I awoke one morning at 4:44 a.m. from a dream. No tainted morsel caused me stomach pain. There was no rattling of the door-knob. Only a dog barked out in the cold, and that half-heartedly, if dogs are capable of such. There was no bright light of an angel, only flickering yellow lights from the city 20 miles away, clear in the pre-dawn crisp coldness. No errant rooster crowed.

It was not even a bad dream that shook me from deep and peaceful sleep. A pleasant dream of the adventurous sort preceded my awakening. It was familiar, but improved upon the childhood dreams where I would leap from a cliff and fly without fear. In those old dreams I never really went anywhere; just flew and always alone and away . . . from something to somewhere.

The only other repeated dream I remember as a child was an odd dream of diving into a huge bowl of Cheerios and discovering too late that it actually was a pool of quicksand in a desert somewhere . . . with no one to pull me out or even hear my voice. Now, that one was disturbing.

While it could have some deep meanings of abandonment or insecurity, it could just as well have developed from my dislike of milk and cold cereal. No need to get too introspective.

I love dreams. I find myself sometimes in my bedtime prayers asking God to give me dreams, to speak to me in that way if He so chooses. And I believe sometimes He does. For comfort or clarity, or even for warnings.

In this dream, which probably took place at 4:43 a.m., I was not flying. I was sitting on the board of a swing, a huge swing with massive ropes that extended way above my head. But, I was simply sitting, not swinging, and it was not out of choice for stillness. I seemed unable to figure out how to make the swing move. I had known how before, but my memory seemed very stubborn. I could see others all around me, swinging easily in the sky, but I was perplexed. Not sad. Not mad. Just curious, as if it were something I knew how to do but was oddly disabled. It did not bother me that others were swinging; I just wanted to join them.

A swing paused beside me and the person on it spoke simply: "Do it like this." And I did, and I began to swing higher and higher among the others. And that was the dream.

Of course, we don't get to choose the dreams that creep in upon our sleep . . . especially if they might be in answer to our prayers for such intrusion. A couple of other details, though the dream was pleasantly devoid of most detail. The one who commanded the swing that descended beside me for the briefest and kindest of pauses was one of my sons, who will remain nameless here. The other detail that was apparent to me was that none of the swings was attached to anything visible. The ropes ascended to the sky and beyond, yet I knew there was no concern. God held us all. Some were swinging higher and faster, but all were moving and all were upheld. All seemed intent and content. I didn't really notice if, in the dream, there were other motionless swings. Someone must have given direction to other stalled ones.

I don't really interpret my dreams much or try to pull out hidden meanings or shaded directives. God knows I need it fairly simply put. Thus . . . swings.

This year, like a few before it, has been a wild swing, from highs of crystal clarity to lows of muffled mystery. But the security of the seat and the strength of the rope was ever-there. And there were a few who slowed beside me when it seemed the memory of how to make it go was fading. They are the sent saints in my life. There were a few who seemed intent to slow down or stop the swinging every time I would begin to move.

Like bullies on a playground exerting control over others, they are so busy pushing and pointing, they are unaware – or don't care -- that their erratic swinging threatens to send others flailing out of their perches.

These spiritual bullies do their damage to the barely-moving ones who are slowed by sin and stumbling or unable to see because of the persistent speck . . . and then they retreat in self-designed satisfaction to polish the well-preserved planks in their own eyes. Their eyes sparkle from the polish, which hides the true color.

Sometimes the festering wounds in our lives can be perceived as willful sin. People fall prey to that perceptive shortfall when they observe in the lives of others things – sins -- they believe would never be in their own lives. Our distaste and disgust can motivate us to some very distasteful and disgusting expressions of Christian "love" and concern. Throwing the right words in here and there, we can strive mightily, not to put the swing in proper motion, but to declare the ropes decayed beyond repair, exercising damage that can almost make the swinger slide from his seat into the great unknown. Then we can say self-righteously, "Why, I didn't push him; he jumped."

It is my hope that we as Christians will truly learn that walking with someone out of the wilderness is more than just a passing exercise designed to make us feel good about ourselves and get us home in time for dinner. The Bible does not accidentally dwell on grace and love and forgiveness anymore than God accidentally sent His Son, Jesus Christ, to die for our sins.

Jesus wasn't home in time for dinner.

We cheapen grace when we frame it in our own terms.

We deflate forgiveness when we extend it within our own limits.

We degrade love when we put our borders around it.

We negate mercy when we place our conditions.

I know I stretched the limits of those who truly give grace, offer forgiveness, sow love and love mercy. But these gifts from above are limitless. And, having tested them and found them true, I am ready to reap from them . . . to plant the seeds of grace and mercy and forgiveness and love in the lives of others.

It's easy for "plankers" to squirm when confronted by the specks in the eyes of those around them. "Must do something about that," is their cry. "Pluck it out" is their advice. The whole eye needs to go. And make haste, for my dinner is on the stove already. Sinners in the hands of an angry god? More like sinners in the hands of a silly man.

I am thankful for a God who has known me from His conceiving of me in His mind; has known me at every stop, stumble, victory, climb, and tumble along this circuitous route; who knows me now. Loved me always, always will. A God who would leave His throne for me, is not inconvenienced by my imperfections, gives me grace for every step and is ready to right the road map. He knows my weaknesses and He knows the secrets of re-design, to make them strengths. And He even gives me a way to bear them as He changes them.

> *That is why, for Christ's sake, I delight in weaknesses, in insults, in hardships, in persecutions, in difficulties. For when I am weak, then I am strong. -- 2 Corinthians 12:10*

I don't fully realize why my path was so fettered and why it became so public. What I have learned though is that it is more crowded than I might have known. Crowded with silent seekers who want to walk a different direction and are seeking God's direction for their lives. There are far fewer defiant ones than we might imagine. Most of the defiant declare themselves so and go on their way, daring you to do anything about it. The others are quiet and dying for you to do something about it, using the tools of grace and forgiveness and mercy and love to pry them free and then the stamina God grants us all to walk alongside for distances far greater than we can go on our own.

The promises of God are not glittering goals to be attained by the ones who declare themselves righteous. The promises of God are for the prisoners. And the ultimate promise is freedom.

> *Is the law, therefore, opposed to the promises of God? Absolutely not! For if a law had been given that could impart life, then righteousness would certainly have come by the law. But the Scripture declares that the whole world is a prisoner of sin, so that what was promised, being given through faith in Jesus Christ, might be given to those who believe. Before this faith came, we were held prisoners by the law, locked up until faith should be revealed. -- Galatians 3:21-23*

Ahhh . . . faith. That other good word. That other life-extending word. The word that moves the swing in the first place.

Look around to see who might be stalled. Slow down and pause alongside. Share the good news that every swing can glide, that every rope can be strong. That every good gift from above is good for everyone here below. Amid the planks and specks, we can still find each other.

CHAPTER 25

WHY SUCH A LONELY REACH?

Where is a voice to answer mine back?
Where are two shoes to click to my clack?
I'm all alone in the world.

-- *Ebenezer Scrooge as a young boy in Mr. Magoo's Christmas Carol*

I don't know if I first saw Mr. Magoo's Christmas Carol the night it premiered on TV in 1962 as the first-ever animated television Christmas special . . . but I know I saw pretty much every time it came on after that. It's funny what can speak to us and when, but as an eight-year-old in his first Christmas without his dad and his first Christmas as a sexually-molested boy, something about that lonely reach spoke to my little heart and it never let me go.

Don't get me wrong. I love Christmas. I loved the years when our children were small and each year as they grew up. The asking changed . . . but the desire to give did not, no matter whether it was a thick or thin wallet year. We had our traditions and I'm glad some things never changed from year to year because those are deeply embedded in my heart and mind and help me now. But still . . . each year I wish I had been more aware of the other hands that reached out and lingered in loneliness, overlooked. I wish I had been more responsive. This loneliness at Christmas was already there, but intensified in the light of Christmas' glow.

Families touched by corrosive sexual sin, who have been almost vaporized by its power to dissolve and break-down what were to be impenetrable bonds often find the pain of separation beneath the tree. If not true separation, then certainly emotional distances that cannot be diminished by lengths of red ribbons or repeated viewings of *It's A*

Wonderful Life or by singing along to *White Christmas* or laughing together at *A Christmas Story*. For some, right now, it just isn't the wonderful life of which they had always dreamed. They might long for the appearance of a Clarence to lead them back home . . . but they feel more like they belong on the Island of Misfit Toys, like the cowboy riding an ostrich or the spotted elephant.

For many, it is not just a lonely reach; their hands are in their own pockets. For others, even their eyes don't reach, but remain focused on their feet. Nothing enlarges loss like Hallmark moments played out repeatedly before you everywhere you go . . . alone.

Some people are alone because they've worked themselves into a solitude through repeated actions that removed them from the lives of those who finally, eventually refused to go one step further.

Some people are alone because they put themselves in positions that are to others beyond forgiveness.

Some sit silently because they cannot forgive others or they cannot forgive themselves and they have joined the statuary in the graceless garden.

Like unused muscles, the hands that once reached out and hugged and granted welcome along with pardon are now atrophied and still. Forgiveness, grace, mercy and love are gifts left behind on the shelves on Christmas Eve at closing time.

I read about a group cast away as unwanted in a place called Blikkiesdorp in South Africa. A shantytown dubbed "the dumping ground," for unwanted people, a place to die. I guess you get to die in peace without judgment raining down on you from the better ones. Is there any comfort in dying unwanted among the unwanted?

I noticed on the Internet a link for "How to Block Unwanted People on Facebook." Easy directions, but, I'm sorry, I just couldn't bring myself to follow the link. We all want to be "Friends," not "Unwanted."

I hope you have it in your plans at Christmas to want the unwanted. I've certainly been comfortable in the past, enjoying my corporate comfort in my nice "stable" job . . . my cozy and comfortable decorated home . . . my comfortable church . . . my comfortable view of my world . . . my comfortable Christmas, insulated and warm, familiar and familial. Plenty of hands. Hunkered down beneath the lights around the rooftop, mid the music and movies, hot chocolate and board games, tinsel and children's handmade treasures brought down from the attic. I didn't worry too much about the weary and lonely hands beyond the comfortable confines of our

Christmas. The red kettle outside Wal-Mart was about as close as I needed to be to loneliness.

"This is the point of no return. What is the point of no return? Just wait until you get here and you'll find out."

Bertram Montgomery Hunter

December 27, 1984

My long-late father's fading yellow tablets, from where the quotes embedded here have sprung to life, remind me that only a few doors down from where we all live and love are those who live without love, or only with the memories of such.

And, if these who feel unloved *were* loved? What would that do for them? Well, according to I Corinthians 13:4-8 . . . . *love suffers long; is kind; does not envy; does not parade itself; does not get puffed up; does not behave rudely; is not provoked; does not think evilly, nor rejoice in sin; rejoices in the truth; bears all things; believes all things; hopes all things; endures all things.*

Wow. That's enough to cause a cowboy to jump down from the ostrich or an elephant to lose its spots . . . or sad eyes to rise and hands to risk a reach.

And what of our churches, busy with holiday plans and programs, special sermons and candlelight services, poinsettias and banners? In Colossians 3:12-16, it tells us that as a church, we are to show tender mercies, kindness, humility, a heart of compassion, gentleness and patience. We're supposed to bear with one another; forgive one another; love; let the peace of God rule our hearts; be thankful; have God's Word live in us abundantly; teach and admonish one another; sing with grace in our hearts.

Wow. Singing with grace could join some hands that have too long been left hanging at the side.

This is not an indictment of Christians or of churches. I just find myself thankful that I have been on the inside, behind the stained glass windows . . . *and* on the outside, among the stained. The views are different and there is judgment in each place. Too much.

"I've fought a lot of battles. Won some, lost some, but I think this is the final one. I won't surrender, but I know there's a change in the air."

Bertram Montgomery Hunter

January 11, 1985

My father drifted slowly away a few years after he left his thoughts of loneliness on his yellow tablets, his legacy a sharing of his pain. Among the words though were his memories of life before the downward slide, in days when he decorated the trees and slid the gifts beneath them for excited and tiny hands to claim. In days when he both gave and received the love that makes this life bearable. The days when his hand reached out and actually reached someone, long before the days when it rose in limited request for a day's sustenance among the poor and slipping away.

My desire is not to make you sad about Christmas, but to challenge you to increase the joy in your life by going well beyond the limits of Christmas comfort to the outer-limits of Christmas where the cupboards of love are bare and where the pantries of loneliness overflow. Where the heart's longing is stemmed by timidity and the desire of life is trimmed instead of the tree.

One last word, and this is for the lonely: the ones among us who find themselves outside a boundary perhaps erected as a result of their own sinfulness still unresolved among others. You aren't truly alone. There is One who is always anxious to take your hand in His, to meet your gaze high or low, to present you gifts and to receive yours. He knows your sin; He knows you and He loves you anyway. And, through closeness to Him, you just might eventually find yourself restored to others and with a less lonely reach. You can reach out to Him with both hands and He will take both in His.

Christmas *is* a joyous season. What could be more joyful than the birth of a Savior -- given by a Father -- who would die so we all could live beyond our sinful selves? Now, if we could just look a bit beyond our sinful selves and be selflessness to others in a season where one self cries out for another: "Please don't leave me alone."

I don't remember how old I was when I received the last Christmas present from my father, or gave him one. It doesn't matter now. He's been gone so long. But . . . I do know he loved to write and he longed to be published. So here . . . just a few words from my father, penned on Christmas Day, in honor of the lonely among us and in hope they will not remain so.

"Whatever night it is, who cares? I'm used to a lonely turbulent life. No one knows, nor would anyone understand. They think this ole drunk is going down hill in a one-horse sleigh. Well, I have a surprise for them all because I don't have a horse or sleigh either one."

Bertram Montgomery Hunter

December 25, 1984

CHAPTER 26

THE WEIGHT OF WHO I AM

How odd are the things of our past that cling to us like empty shirts pinned on a clothesline, blowing in the wind and flapping in the breeze, pulling at the pins, straining to fly loose and either take to the sky or fall to the ground, but bound instead, unable to choose, limited by their lifelessness. They are but pieces of fabric pulled together by thread and shaped into a shirt, a covering. Some of us are like those empty shirts; lifeless, pinned to a stretched line of lingering sin we cannot forget or get beyond.

Do you ever wonder why some things from your past remain embedded in your memory and come up like an instant replay, over and over again, as if, with repeated viewing, there might somehow come some sense as to why they are so visually permanent? It is like if we relive them again perhaps they will have a different ending or a better explanation, as though our vision will suddenly clear up and catch something we never saw before.

We don't recall *everything*, but surely there is a reason for every recall to which we cling, depositing it in our memory bank as if it were too valuable to relinquish. For instance, I can recall my father's smile, yet I rarely saw one past my childhood. I haven't pulled a crawdad from a creek in decades, yet when I close my eyes I can see the pinchers and watch myself carefully remove them from the bacon-bait on the end of the string, like an old black-and-white movie with a happy ending, little boy fingers pinch-free.

My father's smiles and creepy crustaceans are little pieces of the past which factor in to what I came to be, and how I either flap in the gentle breeze or fall to the ground in a wrinkled heap. Such is the mystery of strength and weakness, of pleasure and pain, of defeating misery and soaring melody, of unending sadness and unequaled joy. Of good and evil. Of self-centered sin and unselfish selflessness. It is the weight of who I am. And those who know me . . . or know of me . . . pick and choose and reconstitute at will, coming up with some images I recognize and some I don't.

Among those memories that I replay is an odd one from my middle school days. Armed with a treasured hall pass, I made my way to the restroom, pushed open the door and stepped inside. The lights went out, an arm went around my neck, placing me in a choke-hold and throwing me to the floor. A bigger kid said something I did not understand, kicked me and walked out into the bright hallway leaving me lying on the floor. I sat in stunned silence for a minute, stood, brushed myself off, wiped away a tear I would tell no one of, and made my way back to class and said nothing.

Why do I remember? Well, for one, it was frightening. Two, it made no sense. Three, it diminished me to a little kid in the dark. Four, it was never reconciled; I don't know why he did it. Five, I know I was the victim of whatever weight he bore inside. It wasn't fair, but I couldn't fix it so I never forgot it. It is history, but it doesn't fade with time. It isn't watered down by the millions of memories since.

I was never one to become really absorbed in history. In school, I tended to memorize facts for tests and occasionally got enthralled by a historical shocker here and there, like the Salem witch trials . . . or a queen being be-headed . . . or the Holocaust . . . or the invention of penicillin.

I know . . . those who fail to learn from history are doomed to repeat it. Boy, *don't* I know.

A few years back -- more back than I want to acknowledge -- I was set to co-write a speech for an executive in our company who was preparing to address a group of regulators about the great damage being inflicted on us by what we had determined were unreasonable laws. As we walked back from the executive's office with our mandate to produce something memorable and hard-hitting, my co-worker got all excited and began to frame the speech. He had decided we would frame it around the Peloponnesian War. Snore.

I pictured our boss at the podium as the regulators dozed off and fell from their chairs into the aisles, dreaming as they went down of more laws they could pass just to punish the speechwriters. My co-worker clearly loved history and thought there was no limit to how it can be applied or what we can learn from it. I could clearly see I was going to become a Peloponnesian victim. Fortunately for me, the other writer became distracted and the war was edited from the final draft.

No doubt you know that the Peloponnesian War, which Athens lost to the army led by Sparta, brought an end to the golden-era of Greece about 400 years before Christ. Okay, if you do know that, you paid attention in class somewhere in the past when I was gazing out the window, probably absorbed in the rapidly-advancing war within myself, the one that would manifest into a history that also begins with "P," as in "personal." The tests that come with that one can't be passed by memorizing a few facts and dates. Nor can they be revised as time goes on. Learned from? Indeed. Still, even with the learning, there is often a repetitive process in personal history that threatens to bury us under the weight of who we've been. Can we dig out from the regret, bear the remorse, commit to the repair, find hope for removal?

Regret: an intelligent or emotional dislike for personal past acts and behaviors.

Remorse: Moral anguish arising from repentance for past misdeeds; bitter regret.

Repair: to restore to a sound or healthy state; to make good.

Remove: to do away with; eliminate, as in remove a stain.

We *can* regret. We *can* express remorse. We *can* work within ourselves to repair. We *can* struggle to remove all evidence of the stain of bad decisions and thoughtless deeds. Yet . . . there they lay, waiting for an unforgiving finger to push the rewind button and replay them and remind us of what we perceive as our unworthiness. Did too much to too many. And, as if energized by the retelling, the past roars back into our minds and drags us into unrelenting real-life repetition. The weight of who we were is constantly struggling against the weight of who we are in a tangled wrestling match designed to keep us down on the mat.

We *are* forgiven. When we ask. Which is an integral part of regret, remorse, repair and remove.

Why is it that the unwillingness of men to forgive and forget can so crush the immeasurable grace of God's willingness to forgive and restore? And why is it that our own inability to forgive ourselves outweighs everything and slides in from all sides to suffocate us and pull us down in weakness when it is clear we are meant to soar in strength?

We're *all* broken.

And the truth is, even in our own brokenness, even when we want to take full responsibility; sometimes we're clearly disappointed with God. Like David in Psalms, we want to know why He is so silent when we are so filled with groans. We want to know why He feels so far away. And, you know what . . . He's fine with us asking.

My God, my God, why have You forsaken me? Why are You so far from saving me, so far from the words of my groaning? -- Psalms 22:1

And yet, in a later Psalm, David says:

How precious to me are Your thoughts, O God! How vast is the sum of them! Were I to count them, they would outnumber the grains of sand. When I awake, I am still with You. -- Psalms 139:17-19

Maybe we need to wake up and realize that He truly is *always* with us, incredibly faithful. Even in those times when we are not very pleasing, He is always ready to welcome us back. Whether we are being slammed to the hard floor by an assailant who comes sneaking up behind us in the dark . . . whether we are waging our own inner war . . . whether we are just lapsing into the near-coma state of numbness that accompanies failed attempts at overcoming an unwanted sin, He is there. Whether . . . whatever. And the silence we sometimes think unbearable? Were silence not for a reason, He would be shouting. We just need to trust.

And not only is He faithful . . . but He provides a way out. When we are exhausted by the relentless pull of sin or when we are swallowed up by the waves of temptation that seize upon us or when we are drowning in the discouragement of our failed attempts, He sees and knows . . . and provides a way out.

*No temptation has seized you except what is common to man. And **God is faithful**; He will not let you be tempted beyond what you can bear. But when you are tempted, He will also provide a way out so that you can stand up under it. -- 1 Corinthians 10:13*

Do you think there is even the slightest chance that the temptation feeding your depravity is a surprise to God? Do you think perhaps you have done something so bad and repetitive that He just shakes His head and says "This one is beyond me? I created the universe, from the tiniest cell to the brightest star, but I'm at a loss."

No.

God is only limited when we limit Him to the scope of our own imagination or the depth of our own experience. And even then . . . He waits and He anticipates our turning and He hears our groaning and He heals us. And He lifts the weight of our selves and carries it away and replaces it with His yoke, which is light, so much lighter than what we put ourselves through in our fumbling attempts at self-restoration.

Again, why do we carry these sins on our own, repelling the power of forgiveness? Well, for one, they're frightening. Two, they make no sense. Three, they diminish us to being little kids in the dark. Four, they seem not to be reconcilable; we don't always know why we do them. Five, we are embarrassed when we find ourselves to be victims of whatever weight we bear inside. And sometimes we think it just isn't fair, but we can't fix it so we never forget it.

God can carry the weight. He is never frightened. He is never diminished. He reconciles everything. He knows why we do what we do. He can fix all, in His own time and in His own way. If we trust.

If.

Lay it down, leave it there. Don't say it can't be done. Seek God's forgiveness and the forgiveness of others. Forgive yourself. Seek righteousness. And live. And the angels will rejoice, regardless of what men say or do.

There is one other thing about those shirts waving in the drying breeze. They're clean. The stains are gone.

CHAPTER 27

SORTING IS SUCH SWEET SORROW

The good man brings good things out of the good stored up in his heart,
and the evil man brings evil things out of the evil stored up in his heart.
For out of the overflow of his heart his mouth speaks. -- Luke 6:45

Most of my memories are all too real, but sometimes I like to create one here and there on the assumption that it *probably* happened for me, just like it surely did for all the other boys. For instance, I "remember" that on a camping trip decades ago I lay on my back alongside my dad and pointed into the deep dark sky and learned the positions of the big and little dippers and God's placement of Cassiopeia, Cepheus and Draco. The ground was softened by pine needles, a brook babbled nearby, two unidentified bright eyes gazed at us from the perimeter, the campfire crackled a few yards away and a night bird flew by quietly, though I could feel its wings. And I fell asleep there 'till dawn. Or maybe I didn't, but I so should have that I surely could have. Couldn't I?

I love dawn. Perhaps because I am a rare visitor to its daily appearing. I like how it peeks in slowly and then jumps out at you. Even more, I really like the moon. It seems like it's an "it's alright" nightlight, as opposed to the harsh realities of the sun, which comes so peacefully and then pounces so powerfully. The sun stares at you all day, but you don't dare stare back. Sunset always seems to be a relief. A "you-made-it-again" moment, followed by the soothing cool white presence of the lesser light.

I always appreciated the clear distinction between the sun and moon. One is bright and hot, the other is not . . . and not. The difference between the two is so intentional that it is comforting.

It would be nice if everything else was so clear-cut. The sun by day; the moon by night. Man wants woman; woman wants man. Man and woman marry and live happily ever after, forsaking all others just as surely as the sun and moon do exactly as God intended, ever after . . . or at least until He decides otherwise. Clearly the firmaments were not blessed with a free will.

It never "dawned" on me when I was a little boy that occasionally the sun and the moon encroach on each others' territories. The sun comes up and the moon lingers. The moon pops in before sunset. The first time I really noticed that was when I was 15. I was out in the country —not camping with my dad—but hanging with a bunch of older guys from work who had discovered that a couple of sisters who worked where we did were not exactly wholesome, following in the footsteps of their mother. On Fridays, their home was the all-night party. Their old home overlooked a pond. On Fridays from midnight to well-past dawn, it would become littered with beer cans and bodies, tossed around on blankets beside the banks of the pond. The boys from work greatly out-numbered the hostesses, but it never seemed a problem.

I've wondered if my life would have been different had I mingled on a blanket that night instead of hiding in the trees along a trail that led away from the pond, where I waited for the dawn. I did not say "better." I said "different." I remember waiting for the moon to disappear and the sun to announce that this bad night had passed. But, the sun rose in the east and the moon sat high, only slowly fading. Their presence seemed to mock my own confusion as I hid from myself.

Walking back in the still-dim morning light to the house to find a ride home, I came across one of the sisters nearly passed out on a dewy blanket. She offered herself to me. A friend standing nearby laughed as I fumbled away and I heard for the first time in my life in the context of sexuality: *"What's wrong with you?"* And I began to wonder if perhaps something was.

Those of us who struggle with unwanted same-sex attraction bear a weighty level of condemnation and judgment from ourselves as well as from others that seems to me to be disproportionate to the sin. I know it is because we sin against our very beings when we act out, but I also know that sin is sin and God condemns adultery and the using of others for personal satisfaction regardless. Only marriage fits his design . . . and no one around that pond was married, or intending to be anytime soon . . . at least not to any of the Friday-nighters.

I also know that God's forgiveness is extended equally to all. Jesus didn't die a little bit for some and a whole lot for others.

I've come to see that everyone who struggles with sexual brokenness -- and if you think that term is too lenient and soft, just try thinking of yourself as "broken" -- feels as much pain about their malady as I do mine.

Men who are attracted to men and women who are attracted to women, each looking for something missing within themselves. *They're broken.*

Men and women addicted to pornography lose touch with all reality, hiding their shame and their addiction behind smiles and shrugs. *They're broken.*

Men and women who seek sex with other men and women outside of marriage, whether as curious and uncontrolled singles and teenagers, or as adulterous and wandering marrieds. *They are broken.*

Men and women who have given in to rampant self-satisfaction – masturbation -- are losing touch with real relationships and can't explain why they find themselves more pleasurable than others. *They're broken.*

Men and women who abuse and control each other to show their power because they know they're weak. *They're broken.*

Men and women who hate and fear each other because they don't know how to love and need each other. *They're broken.*

We all remember what happens to things that are broken. Even our most favorite toys just hung around for awhile with duct-taped pieces . . . and finally ended up on the curb on clean-up Saturday. The best dishes hit the floor and are swept away in unrecognizable shards. No one wants to end up on the curb of humanity, so we apply the duct-tape liberally in the form of lies and stories and counter-measures. We glue it all together. All the while, the heart keeps right on storing up the real, readying itself for revelation.

> *For from within, out of men's hearts, come evil thoughts, sexual immorality, theft, murder, adultery, greed, malice, deceit, lewdness, envy, slander, arrogance and folly. All these evils come from inside and make a man "unclean." -- Mark 7:21-23*

Fortunately, we're not stuck being evil. We *can* be made clean. All that stuff we stored up can be swept away. All the inner junk that was far beneath garage-sale quality becomes brand new.

Now in a large house there are not only gold and silver vessels, but also vessels of wood and of earthenware, and some to honor and some to dishonor. Therefore, if anyone cleanses himself from these things, he will be a vessel for honor, sanctified, useful to the Master, prepared for every good work. -- 2 Timothy 2:20-21

So, I guess it's just our lot in life to be either an honorable silver goblet in which to serve fine wine, or to be a dishonorable wooden bowl to carry the slop out to the pigs? Not if God has anything to do with it.

Like the sun and moon each have a purpose and yield appropriately to each other, we have to realize that we can't shake God's absolute sovereignty and we can't shirk our full responsibility for our sins. We have a choice: We can be a filthy vessel that God uses for dishonor or a clean vessel that God uses for honor. We may not be accountable for all the circumstances -- those things that others did to us that bent us or broke us -- but we are accountable for the choices we make as a result.

The verse above says "if anyone cleanses *himself.*" It's our job to do it. Obviously it's in doubt as to whether or not we will. Thus the word *"if."* If we cleanse ourselves. If we come to grips with our own sins and . . . cleanse ourselves.

But . . . what can wash away my sin?

*But if we walk in the light, as he is in the light, we have fellowship with one another, and **the blood of Jesus**, his Son, purifies us from all sin. -- 1 John 1:7*

Sunrise.
Sunset.
Swiftly flow the days.

The days are long past when I can lay on the ground with my father or even my sons and point out the constellations placed by the Father above. The days are past when I can claim confusion or surprise by the sins and consequences any more than I can by the passing of night to day and the movements of the sun and the moon. I'm responsible. Time to sort it out. The good and the evil. The dark and the light. The broken and the beautiful.

You can do it too. Just lay back with your Father – God -- and he will point them out and help you sort and be made new. Such sweet sorrow to see those old things go.

CHAPTER 28

THE PERSISTENT PEEP OF A SEEKING HEART

A righteous man hates all sins, even the ones he cannot conquer;
and loves all the Truth, even that which he cannot understand.

--Puritan Anthony Burgess

Somewhere back a couple of decades ago when our children were still waking up to Easter baskets at the foot of their beds, we bought our first Peeps. Little, yellow, chick-looking, soft, sugary and yummy. They were the anti-chocolate and more charming than a hollow bunny whose ears were destined to be chomped. When you bit inside, the purity of the white marshmallow was almost stunning. It was hard to tell which would melt faster, the Peep or your mental faculties.

Peeps also turn into little yellow bricks in time. With a little Redi-Mix, we could build a formidable colorful wall from the left-behind Peeps of the passing years. They never fade, but they definitely harden.

Now, though probably not good for the economy, we just pull the Peeps from the past out of the back of the pantry and use them for Easter decorations. Though hard, they look soft and can fool almost anyone . . . if you don't get too close. Don't touch. They're brittle and unresponsive. What was once pliable and sweet is now hard and impenetrable. Unless, of course, you drop one on a hard counter. It chips and cracks and falls apart or bounces off and onto the floor.

That can happen to our hearts over time. Something that begins in innocence becomes hard and unresponsive, wracked by the passage of time. The soft shape of a little heart hardens into some other shape, reflecting the pressures applied or the environment absorbed or the lies accepted, until it barely resembles a heart at all anymore. So, we put it in the pantry and bring it out on special occasions. Don't touch or you might find out it isn't really a heart at all anymore. It's just a decoration. Like the Tin Man, we function and hope, but we do it more from our consciousness of what our heart should do, rather than by a risky reaction to what it is trying to tell us. Be careful. It chips and cracks and falls apart. With just a little Redi-Mix, we can build a wall, colorful and formidable. Don't get too close.

Sometimes our hearts have just become dry from the drain of tears of frustration or dismay. Too much pain has been wrung from them and they just no longer respond. The little child whose hope was met too many times with detachment or disdain. The young person whose heart drowned in the waves of harshness, pulled chokingly down into a whirlpool of judgment. Sometimes the heart has become petrified by deception. Or shrunken by rejection. The pliability is gone but the protection is in place. Don't touch. This is *my* heart.

Sometimes our hearts bear the imprint of a direct hit from a well-swung hammer. Each time the heart has wandered away and found itself beating irregularly, there are those who believe it is their calling to beat it back into an acceptable rhythm. Some actually *are* called to do so; others just like swinging hammers and are not particularly skilled at doing so.

"Is not My word like fire," declares the Lord, "and like a hammer that breaks a rock in pieces?" -- Jeremiah 23:29

I understand and embrace the fact that God's Word is a mighty tool to correct us and refine us, and that process often is painful. Too often, though, those who arm themselves with their corrective hammers fail to see that they are doing heart-surgery, not masonry. They wield the words, but when the pieces fall, they forget to apply the healing balm of love and the rehabilitative power of patience.

Sometimes our hearts are shredded by well-meaning bearers of truth.

For the word of God is living and active. Sharper than any double-edged sword, it penetrates even to dividing soul and spirit, joints and marrow; it judges the thoughts and attitudes of the heart. -- Hebrews 4:12

And there we lay, split and torn, thankful for the truth of who we were or had become, but wanting help to find the way back to where we were or on to where we should be. Where is the sweetness and softness that once filled our hearts? What can make them whole again now that we have survived the piercing?

The fear of the Lord is pure, enduring forever. The ordinances of the Lord are sure and altogether righteous. They are more precious than gold, than much pure gold; they are sweeter than honey, than honey from the comb. -- Psalms 119:9-10

This hammer . . . this sword? These ordinances? Sweeter than honey? Not just hard and crushing? Pointed . . . and precious. Sharp . . . and sure. Hard . . . and pure.

Can it be that in its persistence to beat, the heart is both good and bad? Our own hearts and the hearts of those who often pound others into purity from their own purer-than-thou positions? Do our hearts make us both victim and victor?

Bad heart:

The heart is deceitful above all things and beyond cure. Who can understand it? -- Jeremiah 17:9

Good heart:

But the seed on good soil stands for those with a noble and good heart, who hear the word, retain it, and by persevering produce a crop. -- Luke 8:15

So, Jeremiah makes me want to just put the heart back into the dark of the pantry and lock the door, but Luke makes me want to take it from the pantry and plant it in the light of the spring sun. I want to produce a crop.

The answer, of course, is a transplant. Removing the deceitful and replacing with the noble. Finding the good soil and sitting still long enough for the roots to reach into the richness.

I will give them an undivided heart and put a new spirit in them; I will remove from them their heart of stone and give them a heart of flesh. Then they will follow My decrees and be careful to keep My laws. They will be My people, and I will be their God. -- Ezekiel 11:19-20

God loves our hearts. Their collective beats produce a melody that builds into a chorus of His creation. And, like a master conductor, He hears each beat that has morphed out of tune into a peep . . . and He responds anyway, stilling the sound of the many to bring into tune the one. He will do what it takes to bring us back into the choir. Our hearts can be nourished by love or starved by lack of such. They can grow weak from lack of giving love to others.

God placed a unique heart in each of us. He did not pour us into a mold like a sticky peep. He molded us individually in his creative hands and fashioned a heart to make us work. God loves our hearts so much . . .

So much that . . . He will even stop the heart of His own Son. Reduce the powerful beat of a Savior to a pitiful peep and then still it altogether.

For me.

And for you.

In the stillness of our hearts, He speaks to us and shows us who He really is. Yes, the Master of the sword can as skillfully wield a scalpel, cutting away the bitterness and the sorrow and the scabs of the past, restoring the resiliency, replenishing the flow, rebuilding the trust, repairing the wounds, ripping away the walls, running moisture into the dryness. We meet again . . . we beat again. He fills our hearts again with wonder.

Search me, O God, and know my heart; test me and know my anxious thoughts. -- Psalm 51:6

Yes, God did still the heart of His Son because of His love for me and for you. *But only for a time.* And then the heart came back from the darkness of the pantry-tomb and beat strong again . . . but this time in our own hearts. Persistent and powerful, able to overcome everything the world throws at us, even those painful things intended for our own good that can bring more break and ache in their own way than any self-inflicted wound.

The Peeps will go back in the pantry. They're just sugar anyway. A little water and they would dissolve down the drain. A little sun and they would melt into the sidewalk, a colorful and shrinking spot.

But, because God spared not His own Son, our hearts are redeemed.

The purity is almost stunning.

CHAPTER 29

This is No Place for Cowards

I carry the past that each day I chose
One step to another . . . now everyone knows.
It isn't the past I would have wanted to claim
But it is my past . . . it is mine just the same.

I wonder sometimes about all of this
Can there be no exchanging what was for what is?
Will there be no will be because of what's done?
Will yesterday's darkness eclipse today's sun?

Is forgiveness a mystery, a want too far-flung?
Is healing a melody not to be sung?
Is change just a hold-out, dangled just past the grasp?
Is grace to be rationed . . . with some of us passed?

No mystery, no silence, withholding or ration
But clearly and justly and full of compassion
Forgiveness and grace for changing and healing
Are given to us through our Savior's revealing.

Through faith in His love, through trust in His grace,
Our past just becomes our starting-out place.
He is there when we stumble, He is there when we stand
If we rise through the strength of His out-stretched hand.

-- Thom Hunter

It stands to reason to me that if we, as Christians, can embrace the idea that bad things happen to good people . . . then we would be able to wrap our arms around the idea that good people -- even Christians -- do a fair amount

143

of those bad things. And then we could wrap our good Christian arms around those that did it and those that hid it at the same time we comfort those that got pummeled by it. "It" being sin. Surely our arms are bigger than we let on. Surely, there is mercy and forgiveness and grace abounding. Surely we can restore the sinner with the same hope we rescue the sinned-against. Surely God's love -- which is to be in us -- is enough to cover all.

Surely.

We're so concerned with preserving goodness that we blind ourselves to the ever-threatening badness, fooling ourselves into thinking we can purge it, despite God's clear warning it will always be with us. We need to deal with it, not delude ourselves into thinking that our purity affords us some protection He didn't even offer His own Son. We think if we deal harshly with those who have succumbed to temptation that we might find ourselves somehow supernaturally separated from it and unable to fall. Look out below.

We're so determined to flee that we opt for banishment instead of reconstruction. Go weep and wail and gnash your teeth; we're praising in here. We build walls where we should build alliances against the evil that is stripping others bare right before our eyes. Sometimes we bow down in solitude when we should stand in solidarity. We nurse our own little nicks from contact with sin rather than addressing the gaping wounds of those who are being slashed to pieces from within.

> We **all**, like sheep, have gone astray, **each** of us has turned to his own way; and the Lord has laid on Him the iniquity of us all. -- Isaiah 53:6

Did you get that? *All. Each.* If you know someone who thinks somehow he is not one of the sheep; has not gone astray; has not turned to his own way . . . pray for him. His sins weigh as heavily as yours, but his blinders are a deeper tint.

We pray "give me Your eyes . . . give me Your heart . . . give me Your hands." Why? So we can see . . . and feel . . . and do, like He would do. We don't pray "blind me and bind me and callous my heart." Yet we sometimes pray "hide me in the cleft of the rock," but for all the wrong reasons. Not for security and salvation . . . but for refuge from the challenging restlessness of the world in which He placed us.

This is no place for cowards.

This is a place for courage.

Courage to carry out courageous commandments.

A new command I give you: Love one another. As I have loved you,
so you must love one another. By this all men will know that you are
My disciples, that you love one another. -- John 13:34-35

That you . . . *judge* . . . one another? That you . . . *condemn* . . . one
another? That you . . . *shame* . . . one another? That you . . . *blame* . . . one
another? That you . . . *reject* . . . one another? That you . . . *remove* . . . one
another? That you . . . *ignore* . . . one another?

No. Love.

We're not *here* forever: we're *there* forever. Glory. But, while we
temporarily reside in *gory*, with glory in our future, can we not be a bit
less cautious? A little less cringing before the mess? Our knees are meant
to help us surrender, but it is to Him we surrender so we can rise in His
righteousness, not so we can hide beneath His robes.

This is the world, chock-full with God's creation, from yellow butterflies
floating in glorious freeness to hardened murderers pacing concrete cells,
from babies cooing to drunkards cursing, from couples pledging forever
fidelity to adulterers pursuing destructive infidelity, from children sitting
on a sunset beach with a snow cone to children crowded into a dark room
longing for a cracker, from a grandmother knitting booties while rocking
next to a table filled with pictures of her legacy, to a grandfather striving to
picture all the ones who come behind him but choose not to know him.

This is the world, bright and dingy, clear and cloudy, green and gray,
life-giving and death-dealing, abundant and barren, pure and stained,
refreshing and repelling, blissful and blighted, rejoicing and recoiling,
accepting and rejecting. It turns toward us with outstretched hands; it
turns against us with a slap. It heals; it hurts. There is so much give and
take that we often know not what we have or for how long.

This is no place for cowards.

We are much too often the brute beast instead of the bleating sheep.
And yet . . . He is with us always.

I remember taking a walk along a railroad trestle with my sexual
abuser when I was about eight. It was on one of the most beautiful days
I remember. We stood on the trestle overlooking a perfectly clear and
babbling stream that danced upon smooth rocks far below. And I found
myself trusting the one who was trying to destroy me for his personal and
temporary satisfaction. The sadness of the damage done was overwhelmed
by the beauty of the scene in which it had all taken place and the comfort
of camouflaged caring.

There were times in the future that I would wish he had tossed me from the trestle to the rocks below like an empty soft drink bottle. Would it have been better to have forever left the brokenness on the rocks below than to have carried it along on the tracks of life?

God has plans. This is no place for cowards.

I am so blessed by those who struggle in determination, realizing there is no guarantee they will always overcome the temptations attached to this side of eternity. Still, they hope and pray and trust and obey . . . and if they fall, they rise again to hope and pray and trust and obey. I am encouraged by those who climb free from the suffocating mess and turn and cheer the ones behind them. I am energized by the relative few who reach into a mess they do not understand and offer a hand to those whose hands are dripping from the muck and mire . . . and pull and grasp and refuse to let go, even when the slime makes the grip almost impossible. They do not give up; they do not flee; they love . . . and pull.

There is such a thing as glory. We can see hints of it and they are given to us not to make us content here, but to make us intent to enter that glory someday beside those who might never have glimpsed it but through us. Hand-in-hand with the ones who would have given up and given in and gone down into the gore were it not for the sacrifice of our selves on the banks of their destruction.

This is no place for cowards.

I have exchanged the anger I once had for the spiritually-blind and churchianity-bound self-proclaimed saints for pity. What an unattractive flock. Yet, I am aware that if one of them strays -- even into that pure-white blindness of their own self-sustaining spirituality -- Christ will go out of His way to bring them in and keep them safe. Some of them need to be saved from themselves.

Yes . . . I hurt others because of my decades of enslavement to same-sex attraction. I was selfish. Sometimes we feed a person inside who was never invited but has become like home-folk. That sinful guy becomes very loyal, even in his unlimited demanding. He has his own view of the world, and it's based on desire. He is determined to get what he wants.

To quote the Borg from Star Trek:

"Resistance is futile."

Or, to quote God:

This is love for God: to obey His commands. And His commands are not burdensome, for everyone born of God overcomes the world. This is the victory that has overcome the world, even our faith. Who is it that overcomes the world? Only he who believes that Jesus is the Son of God. – I John 5:3-5

Feed the bleating beast's insatiable demands? Futility. Obey God's commands which "are not burdensome?" Victory. Love. Overcoming.

Christ came and died and rose again not to insulate us from the sins of others, but to free us from God's judgment of our own, that being death, which He conquered in our place. And, in His great love for us, He gives us the desire and His strength to work to defeat the sins we still bear. That great love should cause us to willingly bear with others the weight of the sins they have yet to conquer.

But what of judgment? Does it not stand to reason we should suffer and be punished and die a thousand deaths for the darkness we have dabbled in and dealt to others? Don't we need to add a little spice to the consequences? Drive it all home? JUDGE?

Moreover, the Father judges no one, but has entrusted all judgment to the Son. -- John 5:22

Judgment has already taken place. Jesus bore it; my sins and yours adding to the weight. Yes, I will account for all my sins when I stand . . . finally and forever . . . before the King. The King who entrusted all judgment to the Son.

This is the world. The world that Satan wants to rule; the world that Jesus loves. The world that Satan came to kill; the world that Jesus came to save.

Jesus was no coward.

CHAPTER 30

THE SHELF LIFE OF A LIE

And if God cares so wonderfully for wildflowers that are here today and thrown into the fire tomorrow, He will certainly care for you. Why do you have so little faith? So don't worry about these things, saying, "What will we eat? What will we drink? What will we wear?" These things dominate the thoughts of unbelievers, but your heavenly Father already knows all your needs. Seek the Kingdom of God above all else, and live righteously, and He will give you everything you need. -- Matthew 6:30-33

Our dining table sits inside a large window facing west. Our yard slopes somewhat gracefully and a bit bumpily down towards the woods, crossing a couple of acres of native grass and wildflowers to where a solitary path disappears into the trees. This window provides for me a view of how God designed His world to change and grow and survive.

Thirteen years at this window have shown me His persistence. Piles of drifting snow give way to fields of purplish weeds, dotted with brilliant yellow early dandelions. Mowing removes the bright colors and introduces the lush green of the later grass, which will eventually fade and dry and lie beneath the leaves until the snow returns. The winds will come to release the new seeds and return to remove the brittle leaves. The trees are taller each spring and more full. The birds are bountiful, building nests; the hummingbirds busy on the feeder and flowers and then again reduced to a few hearty winter birds that hunker down and peck at the frosty ground. The clouds are wispy, and then powerful, then come stationary days of gray, then absent all together for days, giving way to a bright panorama, sometimes blazing hot, sometimes searing cold.

It's good.

On a spring morning, sitting at the table, having breakfast, Lisa remarked that the redbud trees were more beautiful than ever. She has a view directly out the window. I have a more restricted view from the left at the end of the table and can see only the slower hardwood tree, the one that has yet to produce its leaves. For me, the scene still seems like winter and I can, if I choose, refuse to believe the trees are changing, responding to the life inside them, shrugging off their dormancy, springing to life, rejecting the dull deadness that had reduced them to stick figures on the landscape. After all, it's my view, restricted by the curtains which frame the window. I can claim that nothing changes if I want. It would, of course, be a lie.

On this morning, Lisa rose from the table and pulled back the curtains to reveal the redbud tree . . . for me to see. The untruth of the bare tree dissolved. As I looked at it in a broader picture, with the redbud nearby and the emerging grass beneath, I was aware it too was alive, with little bumps along the branches, like promises.

I noticed neither the redbud nor the other tree was holding a sign. "Look at me, I'm beautiful and better than the other trees." "Look at me, I'm going to be better. I'll catch up." Nor was the truly dead tree I had chopped down in winter to burn in a spring bonfire. "Look at me, I gave up."

I'm not going to go into roots and branches and water and good and bad soil and good and bad fruit. These are plants, not people, but they teach us. Those parables have been presented in a better way than I can do.

What I am wondering about is why we accept so much change in every little facet of God's creation as natural . . . and then refuse to think that men cannot change . . . or be changed? Or, why we think that every man or woman who struggles through the dead of winter and reveals all the twisted and bare branches has to suddenly burst forth in brilliant change like a redbud? Why do we not see the little bumps that appear on the branches . . . the promises?

Why do we hold signs? "You can't change." "You are who you are?" "You've done too much." "Give up."

Why do we want to chop a few down here and there and set them aside for the bonfire?

Why do we draw the curtains and sit to the left or right so we don't have to consider the view straight-on?

Why do we believe the lie?

And why do we tell the dormant through our motions and our words that they have no choice but to believe the lie themselves? That there is no spring . . . not for them. Can we not hear the birds singing once again?

> However, as it is written: *No eye has seen, no ear has heard, no mind has conceived what God has prepared for those who love Him -- I Corinthians 2:9*

I visited on line with a young man in California who said he had believed the lie that he had no choice but to be gay. Just a young man, he said he had lived the gay lifestyle "for many years." It must have seemed so long, like a winter that will not end. He had been told by therapists to accept himself and explore the lifestyle. I don't know if they told him that God created him that way, because I don't know if they believe in God. I only know that they told him a lie. And it had a shelf life that extended for years. His heart would prod him with the truth, but he would fall back on the insight of the blind and pursue peace among the wandering. Recently, someone dared to tell him the truth and declared they would walk with him, as a Christian should.

I am angry at culture for taking control . . . and I am angry at Christians for yielding it. We refuse to see the mold that grows on the lies, turning them sickly green and poisonous . . . and in our own fears, we extend the shelf life of the lies.

Perceiving the struggler as a creeping contagion, we fortify our walls, retreat to the safety of our churches, demand rapid evidence of repentance, shrug at the scraped knees and elbows of the fallen, lay out plans, measure progress, pronounce judgment and rejoice that we have protected the flock from the wandering sheep by herding them into a circle. Do we not understand that rejection feeds the fire? These are not wildflowers.

"He was not really a sheep. He was a wolf."

So, there is this second lie. The first, which sends the sexually broken down the path to darkness is the one the world provides: "You are who you are."

The second lie is the one the church too often tells us: "If you were really a Christian, you would not have this problem."

What a comfortable and dismissive lie it is. Let's just take the moldy bread and wrap it in an opaque cover and hide the decay.

But wait? Isn't that true?

Therefore, if anyone is in Christ, he is a new creation; the old has gone, the new has come! -- II Corinthians 5:17

Certainly.

But what of the man or woman who is a Christian and yet struggles with the multi-layered, multi-faceted sin of sexual brokenness -- homosexuality, idolatry, adultery? Or, heaven forbid, the Christian who gossips, or lies, or judges, or cruises pornography before standing in the pulpit or teaching a Bible study to tell others how to live, or has sex after the prom before heading to church on Sunday, or plans a hasty marriage to hide a pregnancy?

We have so many planks, we don't know whether to build a mightier temple or a stronger barricade.

We like to fill our pews with redbud trees that demonstrate the beauty and glory of God's greatest work. They get the attention, the praise, the "so-glad-to-see-yous." Not so comfortable to have beside us are the hardwoods -- the hard cases that are trying to work their roots into the soil, searching for water -- wearing the bumps on the branches in hopes of being given a little more time to come forth in new life. Maybe a couple here and there truly died in the harshest of winters, but most are just in need of the light and warmth of the Son. We're neglecting the landscape. Many individuals and families -- greatly treasured and loved by Christ, who died for them as much as for the most pious among us -- are hurting and being stunted . . . and it is not necessary.

Like a bulging can, or a piece of rotting fruit, these lies have gone long beyond their shelf life. In our denial of the power of Christ to open his arms to every seeker, we have sent them searching elsewhere into a culture that will tell them Christ Himself is but a myth. Live and let live . . . for tomorrow we die.

The lies of culture and the lies of the church are both in dire need of a recall.

Truth is the fertilizer of faith, and faith is what we claim to live by. Yet . . . when we approach the broken as if there is nothing that can be done for them here . . . our faith falls on fallow ground. Nothing grows. Nothing changes. And then we want to say it is not our responsibility anyway. They're the ones who are all messed up. If you really feel that comfortable with whom you are, you should be more zealous than anyone with helping those who have fallen.

He replied, "Because you have so little faith. I tell you the truth, if you have faith as small as a mustard seed, you can say to this mountain, 'Move from here to there' and it will move. Nothing will be impossible for you." -- Matthew 17:20

Faith and truth are God's products . . . and they never expire.

God *can* use the church to heal His people. But first, we need to recognize the need to heal the church. Instead of hiding from the world, we need to pull back the curtains and take a wider view. He created it all. Christians need to realize that even Christians can be sexually-broken from their encounters with the world. Even the broken among us are in His hands.

CHAPTER 31

SEX AND THE CHURCH: DON'T ASK, DON'T TELL?

"When Christ said: 'I was hungry and you fed Me,' He didn't mean only the hunger for bread and for food; He also meant the hunger to be loved. Jesus himself experienced this loneliness. He came amongst His own and His own received him not, and it hurt Him then and it has kept on hurting Him. The same hunger, the same loneliness, the same having no one to be accepted by and to be loved and wanted by. Every human being in that case resembles Christ in His loneliness; and that is the hardest part, that's real hunger."

-- Mother Teresa

When I was in college, I spent a summer in Bangladesh, working with the Southern Baptist missionaries there. I remember being told the country was about the size of Iowa, but had a population at the time of around 86 million. The cities seemed crowded; the ferries loaded so full they barely stood above the water line when crossing the rivers; the buses packed, the trains jammed full. Yet . . . it was one of the loneliest times of my life because I was so different. Different color, different language, different tastes, different prospects. I found myself too often focused on those differences, forgetting that we all had a desire to be what we had been created to be and do the best we could with where our Creator had placed us.

My clearest memories are of those I saw in moments of solitude among the millions because they stood out. The little boy who trimmed the mission lawn, an older woman who washed her clothes on the rocks at the edge of the river, the man who paddled the boat when we journeyed from village to village, the teacher in the library, the cook in the kitchen. Separated out from the others, these no longer seemed different to me. They seemed very much like me, on a journey, seeking what goodness there was to be had, doing life. They became recognizable.

I think that is how Jesus sees us. While there are millions and millions of us, He doesn't look down and see a crowd in a city, or in a classroom, or on the highway. He doesn't get at all confused by the colors and the languages and the perspectives and the prospects. He doesn't separate us by intelligence or personality or even by good and bad. He looks down and sees the cook in the kitchen, the man at the desk, the child in the corner, the sick and the wounded, the soaring and the grounded . . . and He loves them all the same . . . and each one in his own way at the same time. And He knows we all battle temptations and we all sin . . . and He loves us.

He sees the whole world . . . and He sees my little world . . . all at the same time, and He knows how one affects the other. That's what Jesus does. He can do all things. And He assures me that in Him, so can I. He doesn't define me by weakness; He gives me strength. That's what Jesus does.

But, even though He can do all things, I think those who struggle with a sexual problem -- and there are many different ones -- need to know that there are some things Jesus just won't do. He was into washing feet, not closing doors. He was into opening eyes, not pointing fingers. He was into change, not condemnation. He was into "tell me" not "hide from me," "come down," not "run away."

I don't think Jesus would be very patient with the "don't ask, don't tell" stance of today's church regarding the sexual brokenness of its members. If He were here tossing tables, He would discover there is a lot of hidden brokenness under the tablecloths. Secret lusts, pastors perusing pornography, teenagers projecting purity and crumbling inside with guilt, husbands and wives filling their emptiness outside the boundaries of marriage, upstanding members and leaders combating spiritually-debilitating sexual addictions and unwanted desires.

Actually, He wouldn't discover anything. He already knows. He's seen it before. We -- the church -- are the ones denying the overbearing disaster that our acquiescence to culture is wreaking on our families, ourselves, our Body. We move forward like a band of skittish ostriches unified by our habit of burying our heads in the sand, refusing to address the needs of those around us who are dying inside. We are also the ostriches who won't tell others what we ourselves are dealing with because we are afraid they will treat us as we might treat them. Unclean.

"The King will reply, 'I tell you the truth, whatever you did for one of the least of these brothers of Mine, you did for Me.' "Then He will say to those on His left, 'Depart from Me, you who are cursed, into the eternal fire prepared for the devil and his angels. For I was hungry and you gave Me nothing to eat, I was thirsty and you gave Me nothing to drink, I was a stranger and you did not invite Me in, I needed clothes and you did not clothe Me, I was sick and in prison and you did not look after Me.'

"They also will answer, 'Lord, when did we see You hungry or thirsty or a stranger or needing clothes or sick or in prison, and did not help You?' "He will reply, 'I tell you the truth, whatever you did not do for one of the least of these, you did not do for Me.'

"Then they will go away to eternal punishment, but the righteous to eternal life." -- Matthew 25:40-48

In many cases, the very things that have caused our lives to be so wrecked are the very things we fear will keep us there. And many of the things that directed us down the path we long to detour out of encompass the way we treat others. It is a dizzying cycle and the exit often eludes us. We can become accustomed, hardened and unable to hear, soon unresponsive, dark and distant. It becomes very hard to trust and obey and we become comfortable down at the riverside beating our rags against the rocks, lamenting the treatment, blaming the world for our issues, instead of accepting the reality that the love of Christ can turn our filthy rags into new and brilliant cloth.

We forget that the church is called to be Christ-like, not just Christ-dependent. We're called to do as He would do. What should this mean for the sexually-broken? Not approval. Not acceptance of the sin. Not indifference. It should mean acceptance of the person and a willing, helping hand -- not withdrawn, but wrapped around -- to walk as long and as far and as painfully deep as necessary in the hope of true repentance and restoration through the power of God's grace administered through those who truly love Him.

Instead of leaving the 99 sheep to go after the one that is lost, the church is often busy building a tighter corral to keep the lost sheep out with the wolves where he belongs in his assumed depravity. Maybe he is not so much depraved as just wandering and uncertain and needing the right kind of love. Honest and real. Maybe the men and women in our churches who struggle with same-sex attraction would tell someone in the church themselves rather than waiting for that awful discovery to emerge and submerge them in shame, labeling them as perverted and perverting, if they believed the ears would hear and not recoil in disgust. What is it about revealed sexual sin that sends us into spasms of shock and horror? Are we, as a church, really silly enough to think that Sunday sermons and seasons of VBS somehow inoculate us from the evils of the world? Jesus knew better.

Certainly we can't avoid the truth that often our own actions lead us to such hidden despair, and often our own actions leave us there. We can be too embarrassed . . . too frightened . . . too ashamed . . . too weary . . . too self-loathing . . . to allow the love that some might have to penetrate the barriers we've erected for self-protection or self-justification. We flee from those who want to be Jesus-with-skin-on in our lives. But, the other truth is that many of those who would comfort and challenge and do the freeing work of accountability are themselves restricted by leaders in the church who put protection of the flock above all things. How about protecting the flock by allowing them to become stronger in meeting each others' needs?

My experiences with church during my long struggle with hidden homosexuality revealed the extremes present in the church today. For some, Leviticus 18:22 --*"Do not lie with a man as one lies with a woman; that is detestable."* -- settles it. The man or woman who struggles with homosexuality is detestable, or an abomination. Others fall into the "love the sinner; hate the sin" category and really do little to help the sinner walk free. Love is wonderful and needed, but we also need people in our churches that are equipped for the hard walk that should be an expression of that love.

Perhaps the most dangerous movement in churches today is the emergence of the gay-affirming church. The damage these churches do in their flaming embrace of culture creates chaos in the name of God. Aligning themselves with culture may make them feel cool or sophisticated, but it undermines the Word of God and cheapens grace.

Why are we so confused in the church? Maybe because we have all grown up in the world and we're more familiar with what the world will do to us . . . and we've forgotten what Jesus will never do:

Jesus won't abuse us.

Jesus won't excuse us.

Jesus won't embarrass us.

Jesus won't reject us

Jesus won't neglect us.

Jesus won't avoid us.

Jesus won't lose us.

Jesus won't use us.

Jesus won't belittle us.

Jesus won't confuse us.

Jesus won't blame us.

Jesus won't lie to us.

Jesus won't forget us.

Jesus won't mislead us.

Jesus won't turn away from us.

Jesus won't give up on us.

Jesus won't label us.

Jesus won't fool us.

Jesus won't hinder us.

Jesus won't abandon us.

Jesus won't dismiss us.

Jesus won't hate us.

Jesus won't compare us.

Maybe loving others is reflected not only in what we do, but in what we don't. We in the church are supposed to be like Jesus, but for some reason, we fall short and pick and choose a scripture here and there to justify our actions, rather than looking at the whole of His life. He was consistent.

The things that Jesus won't do are, in many cases, the very things that people will do. Maybe we treat others this way because we at some point have ourselves been abused . . . excused . . . embarrassed . . . rejected . . . neglected . . . avoided . . . lost . . . used . . . belittled . . . confused . . . blamed . . . fooled . . . lied to . . . forgotten . . . misled . . . turned away from . . . given up on . . . labeled . . . left behind . . . hindered . . . abandoned . . . dismissed . . . hated . . . frustrated . . . compared.

Whatever sin we struggle with -- and we all do -- where we are and how we got there is different for each of us. Where we go from here is dependent on something we all need to do: forgive and love. Forgive those who sinned against us . . . and seek forgiveness for the sins we have committed against others. Love each other as Jesus loves us.

Is that so hard for the church to do? Is it too hard to create a place safe enough for confession and repentance to be worked out without the weight of condemnation and judgment? Would it be that hard for the church to do the things that outside ministries like Exodus and its local affiliate ministries do, or at least support those efforts? Of course, the issue with that is, many of our cities and towns don't have a local Exodus-type ministry . . . but all of them have churches. Churches should take up the slack, not *be* the slack.

Can we not look at the sexually broken as at least being as acceptable as the least among us . . . and do unto them? Shouldn't we as the church do the hard work of ministering to our members? Is that not what love is? Maybe we are just too afraid?

> *A new command I give you: Love one another. As I have loved you, so you must love one another. -- John 13:34*

I can scarcely remember a time when I could not sing *Jesus Loves Me.* It's one of the first songs we learn as little ones and it may be those lyrics we will never forget as long as we live. It calmed the fears of our young hearts. Loving each other as He loves us can conquer many a fear and allow us to both ask *and* tell.

CHAPTER 32

LET'S TRADE: MY SINS FOR YOURS?

Sometimes our pain is caused by love
or maybe just the lack of.
Sometimes our love is caused by pain
of someone else's using gain.

Sometimes we're sure that love is real,
or maybe it's just what we feel.
Sometimes what's real is not of love
It's what we get because we deal.

But God loves us though He can see
the ugly stain in you and me.
Our sins, the broken ones we are,
And brings us home from wandering far.

His love removes the pain we feel,
His love restores and makes us real.
His love redeems the broken man.
His love says we can stand again.

-- Thom Hunter

I've often said that if I had been given a choice of sins, I would have chosen more wisely, that I would not have picked from the shelf the fruit of temptation labeled same-sex attraction. I would have gone on down the aisle for some sin a little less edgy, a little less blatant, a little more acceptable, more palatable . . . more forgivable? -- which makes no sense -- but I would definitely have preferred a sin that more people could better understand.

Of course . . . there is nothing wise about *"choosing sin"* in the first place. The only wise thing is to not. Too late. We mature into our wisdom at about the same rate we grow into our sin and they uncomfortably co-habitate. Of course, we confuse knowledge with wisdom, but that's a topic for another day. The point is, we sin. We're not setting precedence, or establishing a trend. Sin is not a fad; it's a fact.

> *We know that the law is spiritual; but I am unspiritual, sold as a slave to sin. I do not understand what I do. For what I want to do I do not do, but what I hate I do. And if I do what I do not want to do, I agree that the law is good. -- Romans 7:14-16*

I know a lot of people have been beaten down by the weight of their sexual sin. I know a lot of people are trying to find some way to lift back up those they love who *have* been beaten down. Beaten down by . . . a judgmental church perhaps . . . a blinded-to-his-own-sin brother . . . a former friend with whiplash from the blindsiding . . . a misguided but well-meaning advisor who has a chart on sin-ranking, with sexual sin being "off the charts" . . . a culture warrior who equates homosexual struggles with homosexual agendas. The list is long of those who are in a frenzied rush to throw the first stone.

Why do I know this? As one who fell into sexual sin and emerged into the bright lights of full revelation, I've experienced the repercussions of wrangling with each of the above. Results? Church discipline and removal . . . loss of friendships . . . rejection by my own offspring . . . beyond-the-chart reactions by the more religious-among-we . . . and claims that my sins were tantamount to a deathly attack on all that is good and meaningful in life. We don't stone sexual sinners anymore . . . but we do pile on enough pebbles to bury them in hopes they will please just disappear. It is . . . embarrassing . . . after all. Christians are to pursue purity, not practice lust. (No argument there.)

So, I was wondering . . . if the opportunity presented itself . . . could I maybe just trade up? My sins for someone else's? Take on the sinful nature of a more natural sinner perhaps? Accumulate a few sins from my accusers in exchange for the one that put them to pointing fingers? My same-sex attraction sin, which I never wanted in the first place, slipped across the table for some wild-card sin of another. I hate my sin and am amazed that God loves me despite it . . . and even in spite of it?

But God demonstrates His own love toward us, in that while we were yet sinners, Christ died for us. -- Romans 5:8

If we were not sinners, God would not have needed to send His son. But we are . . . and He did. Amazing love that.

Still . . . I don't like this sin. So . . . I think I'll trade it for . . . hatred . . . or idolatry . . . or unbelief . . . or debauchery . . . or selfish ambition . . . or fits of rage . . . or jealousy . . . or drunkenness . . . or envy . . . or gossip . . . or lying . . . or gluttony . . . or stealing . . . or discord . . . or judgment . . . or pride . . . or witchcraft (well, maybe not) . . . or "the like," which should pretty much cover just about anything the nail-me-to-the-dartboard crowd might bear in *their* sinful nature. Yep . . . they have one of those natures too.

Some sins are actually greater in the measurement of morality. A person who murders and a person who spreads rumors are not the same. Stealing and coveting are similar, but one, in its action, causes more problems. Still, an exchange of sin might go kind of like this:

"Hey, dude," I would say. "I'll trade you my lustful thoughts for your prideful ones. Even-Steven."

"Wow," he might reply. "If I thought you worthy of my pride, I'd willingly trade . . . but I think I'm probably the only one who could actually bear this sin this well. Sorry, got to pass."

So I move on to the next bargain-basement sin bearer.

"Morning . . . I'm looking to trade all my sexual sin for your gift of gossip. Deal?"

"Oh my goodness," she replied (yes, I know I'm stereotyping.) "You're a sexual sinner? I promise . . . I *won't* tell a soul . . .unless, of course, I run across someone who might be able to help you out and all. And if I do, I'll be *real* careful about what I say. Gotta' run. Meeting some friends for lunch."

Hmmm . . . where to turn, where to turn.

"Oh, hey there," I said to the next guy. "I'm ready to rid myself of this sexual sin. Can I interest you in a trade? I noticed you have an extra heaping helping of hatred there. Surely you wouldn't miss that."

"I know about people like you," he said. "And I know all I need to know."

Hatred leads to quick answers.

"Alrighty then," I said to myself as I looked around and spotted a 'friend' from the past. "Wow . . . it's been so long. You still carrying all that judgment around? Care to unload it for my sexual sin? Something a little different . . . even perhaps more manageable?"

"Get thee behind me," came the practiced reply from a face that looked to the left of my shoulder, eyes pinched to avoid the infection of interaction.

My brushes with Brother Hatred and Sister Judgment were a severe blow to my plans for exchanging my sins for another's. The list of sins is actually pretty long, but everyone seemed more-or-less content to deal with what they already have, familiar with their consequences, already comfortable with their lay-it-all-down techniques.

I spotted one last potential swapper. The sin was not so evident, but I knew he had to have it hidden somewhere.

"Oh . . . hey there." I said. "Wanna swap sins? I struggle with sexual temptation and, frankly, I'm tired of all the baggage that comes with it, the diligence required, the up-keep, the internal battle, the always-on-my-guardness of it all. And, well . . . you know . . . it *is* the worst sin, after all . . . survey says."

He shifted a bit, keeping whatever sin it was he bore, completely out of sight. And then . . . as he turned and ignored me altogether, I caught a glimpse.

Unforgiveness.

I backed away at about the same pace as he. That's one sin I would never trade for. Every sin has consequences, but to be unable or unwilling to forgive? What a burden to bear.

> *Be kind and compassionate to one another, forgiving each other, just as in Christ God forgave you. -- Ephesians 4:32*

I crumpled my list and tossed it aside. Not that I want to hang on to my sexual sin. I don't. And I'm not, through the grace of God and the love of brothers and sisters who go beyond the labels. Besides, there's no need to trade away something someone died to remove. Why trade something when you can gain by His having already taken it away? Sin is sin. Mine and yours . . . and his and hers . . . theirs. We're all mingled in our sinful nature and not as separable as we want to believe we are.

Galatians 5:19-21 -- one of the well-known lists of sins -- is followed quickly by Galatians 5:22 . . . *But the fruit of the Spirit is love, joy, peace, patience, kindness, goodness, faithfulness.* I'm sure you get the picture.

Now *that's* a reasonable trade. The teetering imbalance of sin for the uprighting indwelling of the Spirit. The rotting decay of hatred, sexual immorality, gluttony and sinful on-and-on . . . for the ever-blossoming fruit of the Spirit. None of the things I listed above and conjured to trade for would replace my sexual sin with love, or joy, or peace, or patience, or kindness, or goodness, or faithfulness. No, not one. I'd still just be sinning.

The deal we need to make with each other, sealed with a handshake, heart-to-heart, is to stand with each other and help each other rise to defy the evil one who tempts us each in our own weak way. We can give each other strength through love and forgiveness, but only Jesus Christ can cleanse us from our sins.

I'm not proud to have owned this particular sin. But then . . . pride would be a sin too, wouldn't it?

So, I'm back where I started. As I said, I would not have chosen this sin. In fact, I did *not* choose this sin. But, I do have a choice I can make regarding this sin, just as every one who struggles with any sin, has. I can choose to awaken each God-given day . . . and give this sin away to the One who bore it for me. Why I took it back so often will be a question God may yet reveal. It's not mine to bear unless I dare to snatch it back and claim for myself something Someone else already paid for.

That too, as I see it, is a sin.

CHAPTER 33

THE CONSEQUENCES OF CARELESS COMPASSION

I asked you what was wrong with me
"Nothing," you said, that you could see.
"Just be what you were meant to be."
And that's supposed to set me free?

"But this feels wrong," I answered back.
"Somehow I just seem way off track."
"You're fine," you said, with gentle tact.
"Your feelings are just out of whack."

"Don't carry 'round your guilt that way.
We're living in a brand new day.
There's no more need to self-betray,
"Don't give self-judgment so much sway."

But what of God? He sees inside.
Surely He won't just let me hide,
With self and pride so justified
And truth and grace so well denied?

You answered back with a practiced glow,
"Just drop this sadness, discard that woe,
Accept yourself, just bloom and grow.
After all, God loves you too, you know."

Still, a bit of truth slipped from you to me,
God does love me . . . and will set me free
From what I was to what I'll be.
For God's compassion won't lie to me.

-- Thom Hunter

Outside my window this morning, life is fluttering by. Literally. In the past few moments, a graceful, floating butterfly and a determined and focused red wasp have been gliding about just beyond the window screen. Both of them on a mission. Pollination, sweet nectar, a bitter sting. A mix of beauty and a bit of bite.

Some mornings we want a butterfly to lull us into peaceful bliss. Some days we deserve—and need—a sting to bring us directly into contact with the reality of pain. Sometimes when we want to follow the lazy butterfly down the garden path, we should be dashing down a trail swatting away at a yellowjacket, confronting the reality that life bites more often than hope floats.

I have come to the conclusion that at this point in my life I have been favored by a rationing of compassion, resulting in a reasonable rationality of reality. For the most part, my problems indeed turned out to be real problems for me and many others . . . which in the long run leads me to seek real solutions. Of course, that "long run" has been much longer than I would have ever thought my mind and heart and soul could survive, and it surpassed the limits of others. But guess what? The points of rest along the way were punctuated with *real* compassion . . . the loving-kindness that God provides for the endurance of those who run the race instead of forsaking the pace.

Truly I have experienced the meanness of compassion. That borderline compassion that feels so hateful at the time, like the sting of a wayward wasp, who sits for a second on your bare arm, inflicts his pain and flits away leaving heat and swelling, redness and itching. That's wrong . . . and it's why aerosol sprays were invented, so you can respond in justified wrath. Sometimes, when those who claim to represent God inflict "compassion" in ways of pain and flitting, they need to be shot down so they don't just fly around stinging others.

I have also experienced what seems to be the coldness of compassion. Zapped by truth in its most freezing and paralyzing form, left to drift and die on an iceberg in view of those who sip their drinks on the balcony of passing ships and point at me as I become smaller and smaller as the distance between us grows. They may be cruising on their own Titanic, but no one may know until the iceberg comes into view.

Lest this be seen as merely a meandering of woe is me, I have also experienced the compassion that is real and warm to the touch. A compassion that does not depend on determined distance but on intended closeness. Not on separation, but on walking with. I am amazed at the beauty and grace that some exhibit, pouring out in an immeasurable and constant flow the compassion that comes from an unlimited source. They heard and learned of God's truth and refuse to let the world's definition of it divide it into meaningless portions.

Maybe it takes a mix of compassion. Even the bitterness of detachment can be motivating. Perhaps the experiences we have of being cast aside and tossed away by those who discriminate not between sin and sinner, teaches us great things not only about consequence and condemnation, but also builds our own commitment to convey compassion that is not contorted. I find myself feeling compassion for those who have abused it; those who banged people about the head with love in the name of holy correction. I pity them because they share this world and when they fall, they will want to sample a compassion that rises far above what they themselves have offered.

But who do I *really* feel sorry for? I feel sorry for those who have suffered and cried and were not told that Christ suffered and died so they could be freed from that. And I also feel sorry for those who have been drowned in the gushing carelessness of a compassion that tells them that they don't have to change, they don't have to address sin so they can swim in the cleansing lake of grace and emerge on the banks of freedom to walk free of the weight of who they were.

"I love you just the way you are" may seem compassionate in the minds of the misguided, but it is a hollow statement and offers no hope. No . . . you don't. If you really love them, you'll help them be what God intended them to be. I am saddened for the young men and women whose parents, in their own pain, lack of true biblical knowledge, fear, or just a wish for normalcy, embrace giving in to temptation so they can still have Sunday lunch and smile and pass the peas. Keep having the Sunday lunch, just do it with your eyes open and your heart clear; with compassion void of personal compromise.

Recently, I looked into the eyes of Christian parents seeking direction on how to love their children who are falling prey to the lies Satan is spinning at an ever-more-furious pace and which the world is reproducing and portraying in an ever-more-attractive display. How do we love those who are drowning in proud deception? How do we keep them close and yet speak a truth that often makes them want to expand the distance?

With compassion, by offering the one thing we often withdraw: love.

To love them less with this sin is a betrayal. We all sin in one form or another from the day we enter this world. Self-centeredness can take some nasty forms, but it is still that: seeking the satisfaction of the self. Our response is to be compassionate and giving of self.

Careless compassion causes us to place happiness above healing . . . and we have not because we ask not. The carelessly-compassionate Christian prays for a perverted peace and discovers turmoil; proclaims acceptance and smothers a deeper and honest desire for change in the ones we love. This is not happiness; this is not healing; this is not helping.

Does it sound like I am not compassionate? Should we pick up a drunk on the sidewalk and help him back into the bar so he won't think we are judging him? Should we pause to tell a prostitute she might look prettier in a brighter shade of pink? Should we stock a few essentials in the cabinet for the visiting addict to cook his meth? Should we give a list of topics for the local church gossip to make her job easier? Look the other way when cheaters get a little careless so they won't get uncomfortable when revealed? We may as well paint a bull's-eye on our shoulder to make it easier for the wasp to zero in.

Careless compassion can be as dangerous as not caring at all. I never wanted anyone to tell me that my sexual brokenness was a cause for celebration. Unfaithfulness is unfaithfulness. Sin is sin. Lust is lust. Betrayal is betrayal. Deception is lying. Knowing God's Word and doing one's own will is willfully defying.

Wandering is wandering. If we're lost in a desert and we have a choice between a determined guide who knows his way out or a jovial, smiling and funny "it'll be okay, we'll find our way" sympathetic soul to walk with us until we drop in thirst upon the barren sand . . . who should we choose? I don't know about you, but I wanted out.

Some have not gone with me. Some may never believe I found an oasis and drank. Some are still back there at the edge of the desert telling the slowly-dehydrating that they'll be fine. "Just keep putting one foot in front of the other." Others are standing at the same edge and saying "you deserve it. The buzzards will be here soon."

Jesus went through all the towns and villages, teaching in their synagogues, preaching the good news of the kingdom and healing every disease and sickness. When He saw the crowds, He had compassion on them, because they were harassed and helpless, like sheep without a shepherd. -- Matthew 9:35-36

Don't mislead me; don't leave me.

Compassion is a gift from God that we can corrupt like everything else He gives us. Oh . . . but when it is presented in its perfect form, what healing takes place, what joy abounds, what grace flows and what beauty springs forth from the dry desert, shocking those who view it, like a brilliant and seemingly fragile butterfly that pauses on a morning glory. Imagine, that little fluttering thing that looks like tissue paper in flight can cross the continent and return again. It looks weak, but it is strong because it has learned to manage the currents and soar.

We should open the doors of our church to those who struggle with same-sex attraction, pornography addiction and other forms of sexual brokenness. Note, I am saying "who struggle," not "who embrace."

And we should make it very clear that our church is a safe place for those who are bewildered by the revelation of a loved one's struggle. To discuss it, seek prayer and support and find comfort . . . and love. They do not need the vacuum of silent judgment telling them they must have done something wrong to bring this on themselves.

We should drop the silly jokes and the whispered comments and pointing fingers that we – the sinful gossipers – use against the sexually broken. We have learned not to compound the misery of those who suffer with other struggles. We don't make them the target of derision. We should learn that love is the message strugglers need to hear from those who proclaim such love as a personal identity. We should mature enough to leave our locker-room mentality behind when it comes to sexual struggles.

We should take the time to be aware of those who are gifted to help sexual strugglers and be willing to point the way . . . and maybe, just maybe . . . we should make the effort to learn enough to say something understanding, helpful, and compassionate ourselves, rather than letting our ignorance close the door. Above all else: love.

By this all men will know that you are My disciples, if you love one another. – John 13:35

We should understand ourselves the great value Christ placed on both truth and grace . . . and we should balance our use of them as we minister.

True compassion does not close doors and pass judgment; it opens doors and hearts.

True compassion does not point fingers; it extends hands and hugs.

True compassion does not gossip; it prays.

True compassion does not accuse; it asks. And listens.

True compassion does not demean; it respects.

True compassion does not dismiss; it accepts.

True compassion does not demand change; it demonstrates the promise of it.

True compassion does not correct and reject; it carries and carries through.

And true compassion knows that broken relationships are repaired through the offering of healthy ones.

In retrospect, reviewing the years of dog-paddling in my pool of sin, I realize I would only reach out to take the hand of ones who could see me as I am—created like them in the image of God—and accept me with the compassion not of "love the sinner, hate the sin," but of "I love you as a child of God." These are the ones who went beyond tossing a vinyl ring with verses printed on it so I could ponder as I tooled around in the pool. They had no fear of the water. These are the ones who helped me out and showed me a stroke that does more than just keep your head above water, but actually moves you toward the side. They put more value on me than they did my sin. By showing me the value of me, they helped diminish the value of the sin onto which I held in my distress and it became less and less of a crutch as it became less and less of my life.

Yet this I call to mind and therefore I have hope: Because of the Lord's great love we are not consumed, for His compassions never fail. -- Lamentations 3:21-22

True compassion is not compromised. Compassion, God's truth, love and hope are intertwined like a strong and trusty rope. Remove one and we are in danger of descending back into the mire. Of being re-consumed.

Practice "true" compassion. It's a life-saving skill.

Christ has proven that to be . . . true.